WASHINGTON, DC

great food finds

WASHINGTON, DC

Delicious Food from the **Nation's Capital**

Beth **Kanter**
Photography by Emily Pearl **Goodstein**

Globe
Pequot

Guilford, Connecticut

Globe
Pequot

An imprint of The Rowman & Littlefield Publishing Group, Inc.
4501 Forbes Blvd., Ste. 200
Lanham, MD 20706
www.rowman.com

Distributed by NATIONAL BOOK NETWORK

British Library Cataloguing in Publication Information Available
Library of Congress Cataloging-in-Publication Data Available

ISBN 978-1-4930-2815-3 (paperback)
ISBN 978-1-4930-2812-2 (e-book)

♾™ The paper used in this publication meets the minimum requirements of American National Standard for Information Sciences—Permanence of Paper for Printed Library Materials, ANSI/NISO Z39.48-1992.

Printed in the United States

Restaurants and chefs often come and go, and menus are ever-changing. We recommend you call ahead to obtain current information before visiting any of the establishments in this book.

For Jeff, Gabe, and Miriam

CONTENTS

INTRODUCTION

I often say that a recipe is just another way of telling a story. A narrative of time and place—a recollection transcribed onto a plate rather than onto a page. Be they scribbled down on the back of an envelope or printed in a cookbook, recipes carry the potential to shift memory forward, placing the stories attached to them at the head of the table rather than hiding them away on back burners.

The idea of linking food and memory in this way is not a new one. But it's a significant one, nonetheless. The act of cooking for others shows intention, introspection, and personal journey whether it is one from an office cubicle to a culinary school, or one from a war-torn homeland to a new country. Where words fail, spices, seasoning, and stewing step in to share what otherwise could fill volumes and still not communicate what comes through in a single perfect bite. How we cook for others tells something about us. It communicates who and what has held us up or brought us down. It has the power to show what has accompanied us to the kitchen. And, what has carried us to a particular moment in time.

Perhaps nowhere can this be seen more profoundly than in restaurants. Places where strangers, often unknowingly, experience the personal stories that live among those who spend their days preparing meals for others. Restaurant recipes, like the ones found in this book, are stories with many tellers. Sometimes the plots wander. One teller may pick up where another one has left off. The storylines may be strong and fierce while at other times they are delicate yarns spun as invisible threads only to be detected by a knowing palate.

It came as no surprise that the recipes collected in this book would tell two of these kinds of distinct stories. The first one being the individual stories attached to each restaurant and chef included here, so many of whom are as much storytellers and artists as much as they are cooks and bakers. The other, I knew, would be a story of our great city. A chronicle of Washington, DC, as it is experienced and seen by the community of people who live here every day by those of us who make our homes away from the crowds and the cable news crawls. But what did catch me off guard was when a third recurring arc began to appear. As I lined these recipes up side by side I couldn't help but notice that together they also told a distinctly American story. A story shaped and advanced by what we have come to think of as the American dream. A story of people overcoming hardships and stumbling blocks to move forward and embrace this country, even when it doesn't always embrace them back, while at the same time honoring their heritage, ancestors, and culture. A story that is all of us and part of us at once. Together, I like to think of the recipes in this book as a recipe for a DC seasoned melting pot. This book is a Washington, DC, tasting menu of the very best kind.

Inside it are stories, like that of Chef Seng Luangrath of Thip Khao, forming that strong and perfectly flavored American story arc. As a child, Chef Seng and her family were forced to flee their home in Laos in the middle of the night. Once across the border, they lived in refugee camps before being granted asylum by the United States. In the camps of all places, Seng, learned to cook the dishes from all over Laos, from the other Laotians forced from their homes. Creating the dishes of her homeland became her passion, one that she carried with her to this country. For decades Seng dreamed of having her own Laotian restaurant. She never gave up and now, decades later, her restaurant graces the pages of Bon Appetite and wows critics and neighbors alike. And, she is credited with leading the Lao food movement. A short walk from Thip Kaho is Taqueria Habanero where you can find a different story with similar themes, not to mention some of the best cactus sopes in town. After almost 20 years as a line cook downtown, Mirna Montero opened the Columbia Heights spot serving Mexican street food so her daughters could go to college. Her children were not the only benefactors of this move. DC now gets to experience her culinary gift at the superb taqueria she owns and runs with her husband, and kids when they are not studying.

On the Mall, the standout cafes at The National Museum of the American Indian Museum and the new The National Museum of African American History and Culture shine lights on the only other ways the non-immigrant and non-immigrant descendants among us became Americans. The first native chef at Mitsitam, Chef Freddie Bitsoie, brings his personal experience and deep academic insights to the popular cafe. He also approaches his menu with a love of cooking that began when he was a boy tinkering in the kitchen while his parents were out. I swear you can taste that passion in his food. Walking through Mitsitam as the lunch crowd begins to form, Chef Freddie still breaks out in I-made-that smiles when he sees customers digging into one of his creations. At Sweet Home Cafe, Chef Jerome Grant, a former Mitsitam chef, presents dishes near and dear to him like his oxtail pepperpot inspired by his grandmother's version of the stew. Other menu items, such as the cornbread stuffed trout in this book, grew out of his research of African Americans who migrated west after the abolishment of slavery and speak to why he calls the cafe an edible exhibit.

The stories behind dishes like these often are serious in origin but that doesn't mean enjoying them isn't—and should not be—joyful and fun. Be it the tricked out Fruity Pebbles laced milkshake at HalfSmoke or the Mazel Tov Cocktail at DGS, the recipes on these pages are meant to be enjoyed, loved, and used. While the stories that live among recipe instructions stand as diverse as the people who cook them, what unites them is the desire to tell that story and to tell it through food. They also are linked in the desire to share food and feed others. As you flip through these pages, I hope that you will bring some of these dishes to your own table, that you will find ways to make them your own, that you will savor what is written between and on the lines, and that you will take some time to lick the bowl before you wash it. I also hope you visit some of the restaurants on these pages and that you will allow the restaurants to visit you by cooking the dishes shared here. Whichever recipes from Great Food Finds Washington, DC you decided to add to your own story collection, please remember that each and every one of them goes down better on an empty stomach and with a full heart.

A NOTE ABOUT THIS BOOK

The recipes in this book range from simple to complex with most landing somewhere between the two. And, all, despite their complexity level, were written with the home cook in mind. Several like Bread Furst's tea cake, Maketto's Char Siu Pork, and Masseria's Linguine with Anchovies, Garlic and Parmigiano, are especially easy to recreate in a home kitchen. All three also can be categorized as especially delicious. Others, like the Inn at Little Washington's Carpaccio of Herb-Crusted Baby Lamb with Caesar Salad Ice Cream, or (the now shuttered) CoCo. Sala's French Toast S'mores, require many more ingredients, some serious sweat equity, and a dash of kitchen confidence.

As with any recipe collection, you can follow the recipes exactly as the chefs have written them or use them as a jumping off point for your own creations by experimenting with substitutions, cooking times, and other tweaks. I happened on my favorite boxed-dessert hack this way. It involved a off-the-shelf brownie mix and the filling from Whisked's Brownie Sandwich Cookies, a recipe first appeared in Washington DC Chef's Table and also is included in this book. Turns out the cookie's vanilla cream filling, which tastes an awful lot like the inside of an Oreo, works very well as a thick layer of frosting on a batch of generic brownies. Consider yourself warned. My other favorite go to dessert from both collections include Greer Ann Gilchrist insane Galletas de Chocolate de Amor. While sadly The Blind Dog Cafe at Darnell's is no more (and Emily and I can no longer meet for our traditional "Greer birthday cookies" there) the recipe lets these chocolate chip cookie treasures live on in DC.

Many other recipes in this book can be modified to reflect what you have in the freezer or to accommodate dietary restrictions, as is the case with the Posole from the Mitsitam Native Foods Cafe at the National Museum of the American Indian. Chef Freddie Bitsoie says you can easily sub beef for the pork, or if you want to go vegan, beans. Little Red Fox's Sweet Potato and Fennel Soup is another great vegan (and gluten-free) recipe that tastes as good at home as it does in the shop.

Try to make the recipes your own. If it stresses you out to make a stock or sauce from scratch called for in a recipe then you should buy a premade one and enjoy putting the rest of the dish together. Of course, if it stresses you out not to make it from scratch then you should go for it. Whenever possible we recommend using in-season, fresh, locally sourced ingredients along with healthy doses of laughter and good humor. Whether you decide to replicate the dishes teaspoon for teaspoon or to go off-book, do try to remember to have fun along the way—

entertaining and eating should be fun. Always taste and season as you cook (and taste and season once more) and try to share the final product with people who make you smile, which makes any recipe turn out better.

After you've done the dishes and wiped down the counters, please tell us about your Chef's Table adventures. We'd love to hear from you. Send us a note about your kitchen successes and your favorite DC dishes and connect with other Great Food Find DC fans at GreatFoodFindsDC.com. Here you can keep up-to-date with the chefs we've profiled and see some of our behind-the-scenes photos. You can even post your own pictures of dishes you've made at home and tell us about your stove-side escapades. We look forward to hearing from you. And say "hi" to us on Instagram: @beekaekae and @emilygoodstein.

Baked & Wired

Until I met Teresa Velazquez I thought baking love into your food was something relegated to stories of the animated sort. But after spending some time with the sweet-as-sugar Baked & Wired co-owner I am convinced that she does just that. It's the only way I can think to explain how her to-die-for cookies, bars, and buttercream-topped treats defy the conventional boundaries of deliciousness. That and her extraordinary talent and devotion to her craft.

"After a 16-hour day, when it's 3:30 in the morning and I still have two more trays of cupcakes to frost, I know I could just rush through it and be done," she tells. "Then I stop and think about someone opening up the package and seeing it for the first time and I know I need to make it look great. It's very gratifying making something that makes someone happy."

Velazquez's pies make her—and her customers—especially happy. The Columbus-born mom of two young adults learned the art of pie-making from her grandmother and until very recently even used her grandma's beloved cherrywood rolling pin in her Baked & Wired kitchen. When Velazquez first opened her hip Georgetown coffee and bakeshop, she would put out several of her fruit-filled creations each morning only to find them untouched at the end of the day. Thankfully she didn't let that deter her from making more. Slowly but surely, the word got out and slices started to sell. Today, more than eleven years after she opened the shop with her husband Tony, at closing time it's only the crumbs that are left.

Pie-making at home doesn't need to be an exacting, precise, or stressful exercise, Velazquez reassures me. "The Martha Stewarts of the world have psyched people out that they can't make pie," she says explaining that she doesn't use cutouts or other fancy techniques but instead uses her fingers and thumbs to shape her delicious and pretty pies. "Something about the rustic look is comforting," she shares. "And, beautiful."

While you don't need elaborate equipment, Velazquez does advise investing in a good rolling pin and a pastry cloth. Improvising will compromise the coveted final product. "Go spend $30 on a pastry cloth and a rolling pin," she says. "It makes a huge difference."

She also advises pie newbies, along with everyone else attempting her cream peach pie for the first time, to have your dough be on the wetter side. When the dough is too dry, it cracks and will be challenging to manipulate, which makes the likelihood of getting frustrated during the process increase. If you find your dough is too dry, you can add a couple of teaspoons of water to moisten it up.

"If it doesn't turn out the way you wanted what really is lost?" she asks. "Two cups of flour and a cup of Crisco. Throw it out and make another."

1052 Thomas Jefferson Street NW, Washington, DC 20007, (202) 333-2500
bakedandwired.com

Pink Rider

You know you're on the right street toward Baked & Wired when you spy the hot-pink bicycle that stands in front of the popular Georgetown hangout. The pretty-in-pink bike in question, like so much of the rest of the space, comes from the design imagination of Teresa's husband Tony, an architect and co-owner of the indie coffee shop. On a whim he spray-painted an old bike that belonged to their now-adult daughter when she was about ten years old. Tony added the basket on the handlebars that often holds flowers, and a bubblegum-colored Baked & Wired landmark was born.

CREAM PEACH PIE

Makes 1 Pie

FOR THE CRUST
(FOR DOUBLE CRUST):

3 cups unbleached all-purpose
    flour
1 teaspoon kosher salt
1 cup Butter Crisco shortening
⅔ cup plus 2 tablespoons of
    cold water

FOR THE FILLING:

¾ cup sugar, plus extra to
    sprinkle on strips
3 tablespoons flour
⅛ teaspoon salt
½ cup heavy cream
1 whole egg
1 egg yolk (save egg white for
    top of crust)
5–6 fresh peaches (can also use
    frozen, thawed peaches),
    peeled and cut into 6 slices
    each
1 teaspoon pure vanilla extract
Cinnamon

To prepare the crust: Preheat your oven to 400°F. To make the crust, whisk flour and salt, and add shortening. Work with fingers until it forms pea-size balls. You can work the flour and shortening until you do not see any white flour. Add cold water by sprinkling over flour.

At this point you do not want to work with the mixture much, just toss it until it comes together. Form two balls. You can make one ball larger than the other and use the larger one for the bottom crust so you have more to work with.

BAKED & WIRED CARROT CAKE

(aka Great Aunt Helen's Carrot Cake)

Two 9-inch round cake pans or 12 cupcakes

The cupcakes at Baked & Wired have been showstoppers since the shop's opening day. Teresa Velazquez's Great Aunt Helen's Carrot Cake can be baked into cupcakes, like she does at the shop, or can be baked in a pan for an equally delicious cake. Pile the cream cheese frosting high on both.

FOR THE CAKE:
2¼ cup (11.5 oz) all-purpose flour
2 cups sugar
2 teaspoons baking soda
1 teaspoon cinnamon
½ teaspoon salt
2 cups shredded carrots
    (appox. 4 medium)
1½ cup canola oil
4 eggs
1 cup chopped pecans plus ½
    cup for topping decoration (If
    making a cake you will need
    more pecans to pat on the
    sides of the cake)

FOR THE CREAM CHEESE
    FROSTING:
½ cup unsalted butter
8 oz cream cheese, room
    temperature
1 lb 8 oz (5 cups) powdered
    sugar
1 teaspoon vanilla
1 tablespoon of milk (may need
    a bit more)
¼ teaspoon salt

To prepare the cake: Preheat oven to 350°F. Whisk all dry ingredients. Add remaining ingredients except nuts. Using the paddle attachment start on low speed and once incorporated switch to high speed for 3 minutes. Stir in nuts

Bake for approx. 30–34 min., cake should spring back when touched on top

To prepare the frosting: Using the paddle attachment add all ingredients. Starting on low until powdered sugar is blended in. Switch to high until fluffy, scraping down sides of bowl a few times. Add milk a tablespoon at a time as necessary.

Frost the cake once cool. Pound ½ cup of pecans until finely chopped. Sprinkle on top of frosting for decoration.

Beau Thai

Aschara Vigsittaboot stands beneath a black-and-white photo of a far-off house. It's the house in Bangkok that her father built, the house where her mother still lives, the house where many years ago she perfected the art of Thai cooking.

"There used to be nothing around it but now it's a very crowded area," Vigsittaboot says, her eyes cast up toward the picture, one of several old family photos that decorate the walls of the Shaw eatery. On the other side of the restaurant is a photo of Vigsittaboot's mother, whose beauty and glamour give her the appearance of a Hollywood starlet from days gone by. The captivating photo of Vigsittaboot's mother is not the only homage to her at Beau Thai. The dishes, many done in the Southern style of Thai cooking that filled the Vigsittaboot house on the wall, are ones that have been passed down from mother to child. Her Yum Beef is one of those recipes that Vigsittaboot learned to cook from her mother, and the version that she serves at the restaurant is somewhat specific to Bangkok.

"All of our curries here are made from scratch," she says. "Everything we use here is fresh. Pre-peeled garlic or store-bought lime juice never tastes or smells as good as the hand-peeled and hand-squeezed stuff."

She does point out that the vegetables and garnishes in the recipe do not need to be strictly replicated when you make her Yum Beef at home. She likes to change it up, too. Sometimes she includes carrots, sometimes she does not. The kinds of onions she uses can vary a bit based on what is fresh and available. You should also feel free to experiment this way without worrying about losing the integrity of the dish, she says.

When you order the Yum Beef at the restaurant, try to snag the table against the purple accent wall punctuated with an old photo of Aschara Vigsittaboot herself as a college student. She is holding an elaborately folded banana leaf and wearing a long, striped silk skirt, traditional Thai clothing, she explains. The shot was taken during Loi Krathong, a celebration that takes place during a full moon in the fall. The leaves, often decorated with flowers and candles, are floated on the water. In this photo, a smiling young Vigsittaboot holds the lotus-shaped leaf before it joins others atop the water. A moment in time that now always is part of the present at Beau Thai.

3162 Mount Pleasant Street NW, Washington, DC 20010 (202) 450-5317, 1550 7th Street, NW, Unit A, Washington, DC 20001, (202) 536-5636, beauthaidc.com

YUM BEEF SALAD

Serves 6

1 pound flank steak
2 cups soy sauce
2 cups vegetable oil
6 cherry tomatoes sliced in half
1 cucumber, peeled, sliced in
    half, lengthwise, and then
    sliced into ¼-inch slivers
2 medium shallots, sliced
½ medium white onion, sliced
    into ¼ inch pieces
1 small carrot, peeled and
    juliened
2 tablespoons nam prik pao
    (Thai chili paste in oil—
    sometimes called Thai chili
    jam—available at Asian
    markets and online)
2 tablespoons fish sauce
4 tablespoons lime juice
½ tablespoon sugar
Garnish of green onion, sliced,
    and cilantro

Marinate the flank steak for at least two hours before cooking it by placing the steak in a baking dish, pouring the soy sauce and vegetable oil over it, and then placing it in refrigerator to marinate. After the steak has marinated, grill the meat to the desired temperature (at Beau Thai the dish is served medium rare) and slice into bite-sized pieces.

Mix vegetables together with flank steak.

To make the dressing: Combine the nam prik pao, fish sauce, lime juice, and sugar. Pour the dressing over vegetables and meat and toss.

Garnish with green onion and cilantro.

Ben's Chili Bowl

Sonya Ali holds up a plain brown bag. "It's our secret blend," she says of the unassuming paper sack containing the spices her family has been using for more than fifty years to make the famous chili at Ben's Chili Bowl. A secret that the family guards with pride and love even after all these years, much to the delight of anyone who has lined up for one of Ben's half-smokes at two in the morning.

The Ben's Chili Bowl story begins in 1958, when Ben and Virginia Ali started the U Street chili dog shop with $5,000. It was in the heyday of the U Street corridor, known back then as "Black Broadway." The greats like Ella Fitzgerald, Duke Ellington, Miles Davis, Cab Calloway, and Nat King Cole played the clubs that lined the street and often hung out in the neighborhood at places like Ben's. In 1968, the painful and tragic news of Dr. Martin Luther King Jr.'s assassination broke. In the days following his murder, rioting broke out. Much of Washington was forced to shut down, but Ben's Chili Bowl got special permission to remain open past curfew to provide food and shelter to those trying to restore order. The years following the riots were trying ones for the once-thriving neighborhood, but Ben's remained at 1213 U through it all.

A recent rebirth has brought new life to the corridor and a new generation of Ben's fans through its doors. The restaurant—still with its original booths, stools, and counter—remains at the same spot where it stood in 1958. Ben's also has stands at Nationals Park, a location at National Airport, and has taken over the space next to it to open Ben's Next Door. But two things haven't changed: the chili-topped half-smokes and the Alis' dedication to family, the business, and the neighborhood. Today Ben and Virginia's sons and their wives run the iconic restaurant. Ben passed away in 2009 but Virginia still pops in from time to time to chat with customers and check on the DC food landmark she started all those years ago.

1213 U Street NW, Washington, DC 20009, (202) 667-0909, benschilibowl.com

COLESLAW
serves about 15

1 large head of cabbage
    (about 2 pounds with dark
    green leaves for added color)
4 medium carrots, peeled
2 cups mayonnaise
¼ cup sugar
⅛ cup cider vinegar
Pinch of salt
Dash of vanilla extract

Shred the cabbage and carrots to a fine consistency. Combine all the ingredients and continue to season to your taste preference. At the restaurant, the coleslaw is served sweet and with a little bit of tang.

Top Dogs

On January 10, 2009, just ten days before he took the oath of office, President Barack Obama stopped by Ben's Chili Bowl for lunch. It was a thrilling day for the Ali family, but it was not the first time the family served a famous customer. A long list of celebrities, entertainers, politicians, and heads of state have eaten at the iconic U Street restaurant. Among those who have bellied up to the counter at Ben's Chili Bowl are Bono, Chris Rock, Jimmy Fallon, Bryce Harper, Ted Koppel, Chubby Checker, Supreme Court Justice Elena Kagan, and French President Nicolas Sarkozy.

Bistro Bis

Hotel George helped the DC lodging scene leave its colonial reproduction image behind when it opened as the city's first truly contemporary boutique hotel in 1998. With its über-modern decor and Andy Warhol–inspired presidential Pop Art, it was abundantly clear this wasn't your typical beige-and-brown chain hotel and, because of that, your typical hotel restaurant just wouldn't do here. Enter Sallie and Jeffrey Buben, the husband-and-wife team behind Vidalia, who were brought in to help find the right restaurant for the Capitol Hill hotel.

"After some time, we, along with the Hotel George, realized that the answer was right in front of us," says Buben, who ultimately wound up as the hotel's culinary tenant when he opened the doors to Bistro Bis at the funky hotel. "And it's been a fifteen-year relationship."

And counting.

The upscale contemporary French restaurant housed at Hotel George continues to attract Inside-the-Beltway power players, tourists, and locals-in-the-know with its solid reputation and modern bistro-style menu. Buben's recipes, like this one for Citrus-Cured Salmon with Tartare of Spring Vegetables, continue to please Bistro Bis's myriad customers.

Chef de Cuisine Joe Harran cannot stress enough the importance of stocking your kitchen with the proper tools before you start the prep for this dish, or any dish for that matter. Topping his list are a set of quality knives (he prefers Japanese-made ones like Global, Masahiro, or Mac), a mandoline, and a microplane for zesting. His other advice: Taste, taste, taste.

"If it tastes good to you, chances are your guests will agree," he says.

15 E Street NW, Washington, DC 20001, (202) 661-2700, bistrobis.com

CITRUS-CURED SALMON WITH TARTARE OF SPRING VEGETABLES

Serves 6

FOR THE SALMON:

1 teaspoon orange zest, finely grated

1 teaspoon lemon zest, finely grated

1 teaspoon lime zest, finely grated

1 teaspoon grapefruit zest, finely grated

¼ cup kosher salt

2 tablespoons granulated sugar

2 tablespoons freshly ground black pepper

6 (3-ounce) salmon fillets (skin and pin bones removed)

To prepare the salmon: Start by combining all the seasonings together in a bowl. Cut six pieces of aluminum foil larger than the salmon fillets so the fish can be wrapped like packages in the foil. Distribute half the seasonings evenly on the bottoms of the six pieces of foil. Place the salmon fillets in the center of the foil and top with the remaining seasonings, evenly distributed. Wrap tightly like a package and refrigerate for 3 hours. Unwrap the packages and wipe off the seasoning from the fillets and put them back in the refrigerator until ready to serve.

To prepare the vegetables: Bring a large pot of salted water to a boil over a high heat. Cook each type of vegetable (except the tomato) one at a time for 1½ minutes each, removing them from the water with a slotted spoon and placing them in a bowl of ice water. Drain the vegetables in a colander and then on paper towels. Set aside.

To prepare the vinaigrette: Whisk the shallots, garlic, mustard, and vinegar together in a large bowl, adding the olive oil in a thin stream. Season with the salt and freshly ground pepper. Add the cooked vegetables, tomatoes, and herbs. Mix gently.

To serve: Place a mound of vegetables in the center of a plate. Slice salmon thinly across the grain and fan the salmon slices over the vegetables. Drizzle with extra-virgin olive oil.

FOR THE VEGETABLES:
¼ cup diced fennel bulb
¼ cup peeled and diced carrots
¼ cup peeled and diced small
    turnips
¼ cup diced zucchini
¼ cup diced yellow squash
1 cup fresh shelled English peas
6 spears asparagus, peeled and
    diced
½ cup fresh shelled fava beans
    (outer skin removed)
1 tomato, peeled, seeded, and
    diced
2 tablespoons flat-leaf parsley,
    chopped
2 tablespoons chives, minced
1 teaspoon fresh tarragon,
    chopped
2 tablespoons fresh basil,
    chopped

FOR THE VINAIGRETTE:
2 tablespoons minced shallots
½ teaspoon minced garlic
1 tablespoon Dijon mustard
⅛ cup champagne vinegar
⅔ cup extra-virgin olive oil
Salt and freshly ground pepper
    to taste

Black Strap Bakery

When Greer Ann Gilchrist boarded the bus from Boston to DC, she took one seat for herself and the one next to her for her KitchenAid mixer. Gilchrist packed her treasured pale pink mixer, a birthday gift from her mother, in its own suitcase for her move to DC. During most of her time at the cafe, you could see her using it just about every day in the small kitchen area in the front section of Blind Dog Cafe, a pop-up neighborhood coffee shop housed in Darnell's Bar on Florida Avenue off U Street.

"It was a gift from my mom when I turned twenty-two," says Gilchrist who credits her mom as her biggest baking influence. "It felt so important when I got it. I love that thing."

Gilchrist is responsible for all the yummy cookies, scones, croissants, muffins, and other goodies that were served at Blind Dog Cafe. In what can best be described as the matryoshka dolls of start-up businesses, Gilchrist ran the Black Strap Bakery, the pop-up bakery within the pop-up cafe, Blind Dog, which was housed in the bar. It's still unclear whether

or not there was a pop up microbrewery or pool hall lurking anywhere within these nesting businesses but the cafe did host other limited short-term endeavors like local artisanal ice cream tastings and clothing swaps.

The cafe's name was a nod to the sightless pup belonging to one of the three owners, Jonas Singer. Another member of the trio, Cullen Gilchrist, a former line cook at Ardeo + Bardeo, is Greer's brother, and the third partner, Noah Karesh, grew up in Chevy Chase. Creating a local place with great cappuccino, comfy couches, and a cozy living room vibe brought the three together. It was an experiment rich with mismatched furniture and free Wi-Fi. Gilchrist's soft chocolate chip cookies, which she created with the goal of chocolate in each and every bite, helped the endeavors move more away from pop-up and more toward sit-down-and-stay-a-while-longer. Greer has moved away and the cafe is no longer, but it lives on through her incredible chocolate chip cookie recipe.

GALLETAS DE CHOCOLATE DE AMOR

Makes 12 Oversize Cookies or 24 Standard-size Cookies

2 cups all-purpose flour
1 teaspoon baking soda
1¼ teaspoons salt
½ cup (1 stick) unsalted butter, room temperature
¾ cup brown sugar
½ cup white sugar
1 egg
1 teaspoon vanilla
2 cups chocolate chips—dark and milk (can also use chocolate chunks)

Preheat oven to 350°F. Line a baking sheet with parchment paper (alternatively you can also use a good nonstick tray). In a bowl, combine flour, baking soda, and salt. With a mixer beat butter and sugars together until fully blended and the mixture is tan in color. Add egg. Add vanilla. Slowly add the flour mixture. Add the chocolate chips.

Form the dough into balls and place on the lined baking sheets. Greer uses an ice cream scoop to create the oversize cookies she bakes, but she says you can make them any size you wish as long as you leave about 2 inches between the cookies so they don't conjoin as they bake.

Bake for 10 minutes.

Tan Butter

One bite of baker Greer Gilchrist's heavenly chocolate chip cookies lets you know she has a magic touch, and Gilchrist points to the creaming of the butter and sugar as the most significant step in moving from good to great on the cookie meter. "When you cream the butter and sugar together, it should change color from brown and white to tan," she shares. "Otherwise the sugar is not fully incorporated and the texture of the cookie will be grainy." It can take up to ten minutes to get the color and mixture just right so Gilchrist reminds you to be patient. The final product will be worth it.

Blue Duck Tavern

An oversized black rocking chair near the entrance of the Blue Duck Tavern beckons chefs and guests alike to stop, lean back, and rock for a while. This level of inviting comfort comes through in the feel and ease in the menus offered at Blue Duck Tavern, a Michelin-starred restaurant with an open kitchen and simple yet pretty contemporary Shaker design.

All the chefs that have led the kitchen at the popular restaurant have built their menus around fresh flavors, local ingredients, and reimagined American cuisine. Recipes like the Poached Egg with Field Mushroom Ragout & Foie Gras continue to show why the restaurant housed in the Hyatt is among the city's favorite brunch splurges.

The Blue Duck's pastry program exhibits a similar level of ease and expertise at the West End eatery, widely pointed to for serving some of the best restaurant desserts in town. The pastry chefs here use ingredients from a group of hand-picked suppliers. For the BDT Strawberry Shortcake, only strawberries that are red throughout are allowed and the payoff can be savored in every last bite of the divine final product. Not ordering some of his homemade ice cream to accompany it can be considered an act of subversion. Try the strawberry ice cream when it too is in season. It may even contain some of the fruit from the patch in the garden that frames the outdoor patio.

1201 24th Street NW, Washington, DC 20037, (202) 419-6755, blueducktavern.com

POACHED EGG WITH FIELD MUSHROOM RAGOUT & FOIE GRAS

Serves 4

FOR THE MUSHROOM RAGOUT:
¼ pound shiitake mushrooms
¼ pound oyster mushrooms
¼ cup blended oil
1 garlic clove
1 fresh sprig of thyme, which
    seasonally can be found
    growing in Blue Duck
    Tavern's outdoor herb garden)
¼ cup heavy cream
3 ounces mushroom ragout
1 fresh egg
½ ounce foie gras terrine
1 slice country top bread
1 teaspoon butter
Black pepper
3 shaved black truffles

Special equipment: A small cast-iron pot (an individual-size Le Creuset pot works well)

To prepare the mushroom ragout: Preheat the oven to 350°F. Wash and dice the mushrooms. Mix the mushrooms with the oil, garlic, and thyme. Place on a sheet pan and cook in the oven for 10 minutes. Remove and let mushrooms cool. Once cooled, chop the mushrooms. Add the cream and cook for 10 minutes. Cool down and store in refrigerator.

To assemble: Warm the mushroom ragout and place into a small cast-iron pot. Crack the egg on top of the ragout and then place into a double boiler and cover. Cook until the egg is medium, and then remove the pot from the double boiler. Cut the foie gras into a half moon and place next to the egg.

Toast the bread and spread the butter on top. Cut the bread into 4 batonette pieces and stack next to the cast–iron pot. Season with cracked black pepper and black truffles. Serve.

BDT STRAWBERRY SHORTCAKE

Serves 8–10

6 ounces cake flour
6 ounces all-purpose flour
¼ cup sugar
2 teaspoons baking powder
2 teaspoons salt
½ teaspoon baking soda
4 ounces (1 stick) unsalted butter
1 cup buttermilk
½ cup heavy cream
Grated rind of 1 orange

FOR THE STRAWBERRIES:
2 pints fresh strawberries
¼ cup granulated sugar
2 tablespoons Grand Marnier
    (optional)
2 cups heavy cream
¼ cup confectioners sugar

Preheat the oven to 400°F. Mix all the dry ingredients. Cut the butter into the flour with a pastry blender or the tips of your fingers so it resembles coarse meal. Stir in the buttermilk, cream, and orange rind quickly, being careful not to overmix.

Portion into 3-inch dessert rings on a greased cookie sheet using an ice cream scoop.

Bake until browned and cooked through, about 15 minutes. Cool.

Wash, hull, and slice 2 pints of fresh strawberries. Sprinkle with ¼ cup sugar (or to taste) and 2 tablespoons of Grand Marnier (optional). Whip 2 cups heavy cream with ¼ cup confectioners sugar.

Split the biscuits in half and fill with the marinated strawberries. Top with whipped cream.

Boqueria Dupont Circle

When I picture Chef Marc Vidal's family tree, I imagine it planted right alongside a restaurant, providing shade to what can easily be considered his family's business. Growing up in Barcelona, Vidal's grandfather owned a restaurant and later on his mother and aunt bought an eatery of their own called Roca, where they served traditional Spanish dishes for twenty years. Roca was Vidal's home—and kitchen—away from home.

"In the morning I would go with my mom to help her open," he happily recalls what was the daily routine from the time he was six years old until he was sixteen. "I would make coffee and bread and Spanish omelets. Then after school I would go back to be with my mom and help some more."

Vidal started culinary school at sixteen and his career path took him from Spain to France to Miami—with a few other stops along the way. From Miami he moved up north to Boqueria, first in New York and then here, bringing with him a creative spin on the beloved Spanish cuisine inspired by the kind of cooking his mom and grandfather used to do back home.

The Fideua Negra served at the Dupont Circle restaurant is one of those dishes. "My family ate it all the time on Sundays by the beach," he tells. "This version is like the classic dish but with squid ink."

When attempting his recipe at home, Vidal stresses the importance of letting the sofrito cook for a long, long time. The recipe calls for two hours but if you can let it go for six hours it will be that much better and well worth the sweat equity and time, he tells. The chef also wants the home cook to know that a paella pan really is necessary to make this dish, but if you want to use a premade lobster or fish stock you can, although, of course, homemade is almost always better and will make the dish that much more flavorful. If you can find a beach to stare at as you eat, it's a pretty safe bet it will taste even better.

1837 M Street NW, Washington, DC 20036, (202) 558-9545, boqueriadc.com

FIDEUA NEGRA
(SQUID INK FIDEO)

Serves 1

FOR THE LOBSTER STOCK:*
2 lobster heads, cut in half
2 tablespoons canola oil
½ Spanish onion, chopped
1 carrot, peeled and finely
    chopped
2 garlic cloves, skin on
1 leek, finely chopped
1 teaspoon sweet paprika
3 plum tomatoes, roughly
    chopped
½ cup brandy
½ cup white wine
Water to cover (about 2 quarts)
1 tablespoon tomato paste
4 tablespoons squid ink
*Store-bought lobster or fish
    stock can be used instead of
    homemade.

Special equipment: Paella pan

To prepare the lobster stock: Sauté the lobster heads in a large pot with the canola oil over medium heat. Cook until the lobster is caramelized. Remove the lobster from the pot and set aside.

In the same pot, sweat the onions, carrots, garlic and leeks for 10 minutes over medium heat. Add the sweet paprika and sweat without burning for 30 seconds, until fragrant. Add the tomatoes and cook for 5 minutes. Add the brandy and flambé. Add the white wine and cook until reduced by half.

Place the lobster back into the pot, add water and bring to a boil. Let simmer for 1 hour. Remove from the heat and let infuse for 2 hours. After two hours, strain through a fine chinoise. Mix the stock with the squid ink and stir until it is combined.

To prepare the sofrito: Start by heating the olive oil in a pan over medium heat. Cut the onions and garlic in small dice and cook in the pan until translucent. Add the tomatoes and continue to cook for 30 minutes. Add the sepia and reduce the heat to low, cooking for approximately 2 more hours until the sofrito is caramelized and has a consistency of marmalade. Cook uncovered.

To prepare the fideua: Preheat the oven to 450°F. In a paella pan, sear the shrimp on both sides and set aside. Add the sofrito to the pan and sauté for 1 minute. Add the fideo noodles and stir to combine with the sofrito. Add the boiling stock and salt to taste. Cook for about 5 minutes on high and then place the manila clams and the shrimp on top. Place in the oven at 450°F for about 5 more minutes. Remove when fideos are crispy on top and the liquid is gone. Drizzle with olive oil and place on the stove over high heat for a minute. During this time the "socarrat" or crispy bottom will form. Serve with a piece of lemon on the side and topped with a tablespoon of garlic aioli and a sprinkle of chives.

FOR THE SOFRITO:
Olive oil, a small amount to coat the pan
2 onions
2 garlic cloves
2 tomatoes, grated
1 large sepia (cuttlefish) cut in ½-inch dice
3 ruby red shrimp
1 tablespoon sofrito
1 cup small fideo noodles (pre-toasted in the oven at 350°F for about 7–10 minutes until golden brown)
12 ounces lobster stock*
Salt to taste
4 manila clams
Olive oil for drizzling
1 tablespoon garlic aioli (store-bought is fine)
Chopped chives for garnish

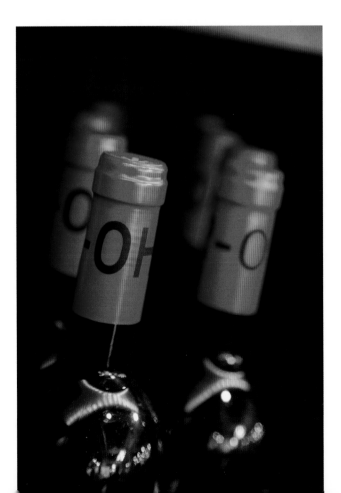

Bourbon Steak

Chef Adam Sobel's flavorful salmon burger seamlessly brings together an array of components like his house-made kimchee, delicate ginger, and chili paste. Although each of these pieces is an essential part of the whole dish, it's the salmon's sourcing that the chef says makes or breaks the integrity of the final product. Whenever possible Sobel uses wild arctic char for the recipe, but points to trout as a great replacement if you can't find good salmon. What he does warn against using in this non-beef burger is farmed Atlantic salmon.

"Stay away from Atlantic farm-raised salmon," he says adding that much to the delight of many a chef, including himself, more customers are asking and are aware of the sourcing of all ingredients especially fish. "There are lots of nasty things associated with Atlantic farm-raised salmon. And, it doesn't taste good."

If you do go the trout route with this burger recipe, keep in mind that trout has less of a fat content than salmon, which you need to account for as you cook it. Sobel recommends cooking the trout to about a medium rare and notes that once you take it out it will carry over (or continue cooking) to a medium well. At Bourbon Steak, all the fabulous kimchee is made in house. At any given moment the chef always has a huge amount of it fermenting and goes through about a hundred pounds of cabbage a week. For those who don't have the time or space to do that at home, you can purchase some great premade kimchee at local Korean markets. But if you are on the fence about attempting to make the traditional fermented condiment at home, Sobel encourages you to go for it. He promises it's not that hard. Like so many other things in life, the most challenging part is waiting. "The longer it goes, the more depth of flavor," he says.

Adam Sobel left Bourbon Steak for the west coast in 2012, but thankfully left behind the Salmon Burger.

2800 Pennsylvania Avenue NW, Washington, DC 20007, (202) 944-2026, bourbonsteakdc.com

THE JEFFERSON COCKTAIL
Makes 1 Cocktail

2 ounces bourbon (like Bulleit)
¾ ounce Carpano Antica
    (an Italian sweet vermouth)
½ ounce crème de mûre
    (a blackberry liqueur, not
    blackberry brandy)
1 dash Old Fashioned Bitters
    (like Fee Bros)
Lemon zest

Combine all ingredients in a mixing glass and stir until well chilled (about 20 seconds). Strain into a chilled coupe or martini glass. Garnish with a wide swath of lemon zest.

SALMON OR ARCTIC CHAR BURGER

Makes 1 Burger

FOR THE GINGER AIOLI:
1 tablespoon chopped shallot
6 tablespoons chopped ginger
1 tablespoon Dijon mustard
2 egg yolks
½ cup grape-seed oil
½ cup olive oil
2 ounces ginger, microplaned
½ lemon, juiced

FOR THE KOCHUJANG SAUCE:
½ cup kochujang paste
   (sun-dried Korean chili paste)
1½ cups water
½ cup apple cider vinegar
1 cup sugar
1 tablespoon sesame seeds
   (toasted)
1 tablespoon sesame oil
1 lemon, juiced

Special equipment: fish spatula and palette knife

To prepare the ginger aioli: Mix the shallots, chopped ginger, Dijon, and egg yolks in a blender and puree until it's a smooth, slightly aerated consistency. Slowly pour in the grape-seed oil, followed by the olive oil, to create an emulsion. Remove from blender and transfer to a large bowl. Once in bowl, mix all the ingredients together. Mix in the microplaned ginger. Fold the juice of half a lemon into the completed ginger aioli. The lemon juice helps brighten and bring out the flavors of the aioli.

To prepare the kochujang sauce: Combine all the ingredients in a bowl and mix.

To prepare the burgers: Lather the salmon filet on both sides with olive oil and season with salt, pepper, and espelette. Place the salmon on the baking sheet skin side up and place in the broiler for 2 minutes. Flip the fish over and cook for another 2 minutes. At this point your fish fillet should be at about medium rare. Brush on a light coating of the kochujang sauce and place back into the broiler and cook until medium with a slightly charred crust of the kochujang sauce.

Remove the fillet from the heat and let it rest for a minute while toasting the bun. Once the buns are perfectly toasted, spread a layer of the ginger aioli on both sides of the bun. On the top half of the bun, layer the toppings in the following order: cilantro, kimchee, jalapeño, and cucumber. Place the salmon fillet on the bottom half of the bun and place the top half of the bun with all the accompaniments on top of the salmon fillet. Garnish with a pickle spear.

FOR THE BURGER:

4-ounce portion of salmon when in season (char is a suitable substitute)

Olive oil

Salt and pepper to taste

Ground espelette (a French chili pepper)

Kochujang sauce (recipe below)

Sesame-seed bun

Ginger aioli (recipe below)

Cilantro

Kimchee (found at your local Asian specialty store or made in house)

Red and green jalapeño (sliced very thin)

English cucumbers

Pickle spear

Brasserie Beck

When Brasserie Beck first opened, Chef Robert Wiedmaier couldn't help but laugh just a little bit every time someone came up to him and remarked how he'd stumbled on something new. "There was nothing that novel about it," he says about the concept of a brasserie. "They are all over Europe. They are all over San Francisco. They are all over New York."

Where they were not all over was Washington, DC. And, that, was what made his venture a novel one—and still does. Before Wiedmaier opened the doors to Brasserie Beck, you would be hard pressed to find a place inside the Beltway where you could order moules and frites, along with an international beer from a list a hundred bottles long.

When it comes to the mussels at Beck, and all the seafood he serves for that matter, Wiedmaier goes to great lengths to ensure its quality and safety. The chef lists the origins of all the fruits of the sea he uses on his menus and even went down to Louisiana after the oil spill cleanup to see firsthand how the supply had rebounded. "I went down there with the USDA, the director of EPA, and representatives from the White House," he shares. "We went fishing. We ate the food. It all looked and tasted great."

For those who get a bit nervous about purchasing fresh seafood here at home, the chef first recommends finding a vendor who is very busy and moving product off the shelves. "It's just like a sushi restaurant," he tells. "You don't want to go to one that isn't packed."

Once you settle on a shop or fishmonger that make you feel comfortable, the chef says the best tools you can bring shopping are your senses. "The first thing I do with any seafood is smell it," he shares. "If it doesn't smell like the ocean or water, don't buy it. It's supposed to smell nice and sweet like the ocean. Then I look at it. If the eyes are cloudy it's not good."

1101 K Street NW, Washington, DC 20005, (202) 408-1717, beckdc.com

PROVENÇAL MUSSELS WITH TOMATO, GARLIC, CAPERS & BASIL

Serves 1

2 peeled, sliced shallots
2 tablespoons chopped garlic
1 tablespoon olive oil
1 pound, cleaned, scrubbed,
  de-bearded PEI mussels
  (leave in shell)
½ cup diced plum tomatoes
½ cup dry white wine or
  vermouth
2 tablespoons capers
1 teaspoon ground espelette
  pepper
2 tablespoons chopped small-
  leaf basil
1 whole garlic bulb
Fresh baguette
Fresh parsley for garnish

In a pot or heavy pan, sweat shallots and chopped garlic in olive oil. Add mussels, tomatoes, white wine, capers, pepper, and basil. Cover with lid and cook until mussels open up.

Take one whole bulb of garlic, wrap in foil and cook in 300°F oven until soft (about 30-40 minutes). Remove from oven, cut in half, and rub on slices of grilled or toasted baguette.

Cooked mussels can be eaten right from the pot or pan or transferred to a wide-rim soup bowl. Use baguette slices to soak up mussel broth. Top with chopped fresh parsley and serve with a good Chardonnay or Sauvignon Blanc.

Bread Furst

Mark Furstenberg stops for a moment in the light-filled pastry kitchen of Bread Furst, the Parisian-style neighborhood bakery he opened in 2014. He smiles, and then, as croissant dough is being prepped behind him, shares the tale of his first professional baking experience. As the James Beard award winner speaks, it's hard not to consider the contrast between the place he is describing in the story and the place where he now stands. It is a contrast that is as charming as Bread Furst itself.

"I was 19 and I got a job as an assistant cook at a boy's camp in Vermont," tells the Master Baker. "The head cook got sick and I was left to cook for 150 boys and counselors. So I hitchhiked into town and bought a cookbook, a Better Homes and Gardens book, and baked cornbread and biscuits. I also made some yeasted breads."

Decades after his turn in the summer camp mess, Furstenberg brought fresh bread to a city subsisting on frozen bagels and sliced Wonder from the grocery store -- first Marvelous Market and later with BreadLine. Both establishments helped transform the city's food culture. In the early days of Marvelous Market, the shop was so popular that there was a two-baguette minimum and lines typically stretched out of the store. The now shuttered market stood just up the street from Politics and Prose, the DC cultural landmark co-founded by his sister Carla Cohen, and is only about a half-mile from Bread Furst's Van Ness location.

Until he started Marvelous Market in 1990, Furstenberg had been an enthusiastic home baker with a series of very real day jobs that had nothing to do with cooking. "When I decided to open Marvelous Market it was because of the void—I felt that there was no good bread in Washington," he says.

In addition to gorgeous breads, Bread Furst sells its version of rustic well-loved and well-baked, flaky croissants, seasonal fruit pies, hand-glazed donuts, as well as other beloved pastries. The French influence is apparent but the true focus is on flavor and not on creating baked goods that look perfect but taste far from it.

"French pastries are admired," he says. "American pastries are loved. The American heart belongs to American pastry."

Furnstenberg designed Bread Furst with three separate kitchens: a bread kitchen, a savory kitchen and a pastry kitchen. All are staffed with talent he has brought in. It is his hope that his bakers, like Executive Pastry Chef Cecile Mouthon who created the Seasonal Fruit Tea Cake recipe, will take over the bakery as owners when he fully retires.

For Mouthon, spending her days in a bakery is a bit like going home again. Mouthon's grandfather was a baker in France who owned a small bakeshop that mostly sold fresh breads, croissants, and other types of morning pastries. The trained pastry chef regularly traveled with her parents and sister to visit her grandparents in France. "All of my childhood memories involve baking," she explains. "I remember visiting him when I was in third grade and asking my grandfather to wake me up at 4 am so I can do croissants with him."

As a seasonal bakery, Bread Furst's offerings change year round. Mouthon's earthy but not overly sweet tea cake is one of the few items that she and her team bake year round with only the fruit changing to reflect the season. It's also a recipe that she says most home cooks can tackle, even those who might be shy around pastry and bread.

"It's as foolproof as anything gets in baking," she promises.

4434 Connecticut Ave., NW, Washington, DC 20008, breadfurst.com

SEASONAL FRUIT TEA CAKE

2 blood oranges or any citrus
 fruit available, zested, and
 segmented
1 cup sugar
1½ cups all-purpose flour
2 teaspoons baking powder
¼ teaspoons salt
½ cup full-fat Greek yogurt
3 eggs
2 teaspoons vanilla extract
½ cup olive oil

Combine zest from oranges with sugar and rub together to infuse sugar with flavor from zest. Sift together flour, baking powder, and salt. In a bowl, combine sugar with yogurt and mix until combined. Add eggs and vanilla extract to yogurt/sugar mixture, being sure to scrape the bottom of the bowl. Be careful not over mix. Add dry ingredients. Stream in olive oil and mix, incorporating the olive oil fully. Put in desired receptacle, layer fruit on top, and bake at 350°F until toothpick comes out clean

Tested fruit rotations include: Raspberries, plums, rhubarb, blueberries and strawberries. When using fruit other than oranges, omit the orange zest and substitute with a complimentary zest of another citrus fruit.

Note: As with all quick breads (non-yeast) breads, it's important not to over mix.

Cakelove

Warren Brown knows how to keep a promise.

When he first started baking, Brown was frustrated by the need to find the right recipe in the right cookbook on the right page every single time he wanted to create something new. "I remember thinking I couldn't wait for the day when I didn't need to open a cookbook anymore, for the time when I could just recite a recipe off the top of my head," recalls the Cakelove founder and owner. "It was a little promise I made to myself that I would get to that point. The whole business really is a promise I made to myself."

Six shops and more than ten years later, the litigator-turned-baker has more than kept his word. Brown can rattle off recipes the way most people do their own phone number, and his story of leaving a promising legal career to pursue his buttercream dreams has landed him on The Oprah Winfrey Show, American Express commercials, and several other high-profile media gets. His sugar-and-flour empire sells slews of beloved cakes, cookies, and cupcakes each week and Cakelove now stands as something of a DC institution with multiple locations around town. All of his baked goods, like his Susie's a Pink Lady, are also known for using only natural ingredients for coloring instead of dyes or food coloring. In the case of Susie, it's raspberries—lots and lots of fresh raspberries—that create its pretty pink hue.

Brown first baked the cake for a friend's birthday party whose name was, wait for it . . . Susie. The original creation was a classic French genoise, but once he started making it at the bakery he quickly discovered that the American palate preferred a moister cake like the ones made from boxed mixes so many grew up on. It's now a vanilla butter layer cake with raspberry buttercream. For those attempting Susie at home, Brown recommends always making sure there is buttercream on top and on bottom, sandwiching the berries. "Berries hitting the cake doesn't look good," he shares. He also suggests taking the time to line all the berries up so they are facing the same direction. "This is a beautiful cake to bake and serve. It's a fair amount of work and the labor of love shows with all of the colors and flavors that jump out with every slice," he says. "Fresh raspberries make a great statement, so pack the middle layers with them."

It is an eye toward this level of detail that clearly has helped him keep his sweet promise from a decade ago.

A word of help from Brown on the batter: "The cake is a relatively loose batter that will not look homogenous at the final mix. That's intentional. There is a fairly large amount of fat relative to the starch in the cake, which is necessary to balance the proteins from the all-purpose flour. The potato starch is a must; do not skip it or substitute cornstarch. Potato starch can be found easily in specialty baking aisles at your local grocer. The buttercream is not difficult to make, but requires the proper equipment. A candy thermometer and stand mixer are very helpful to have."

Cakelove is no longer but the Susie's a Pink Lady Layer Cake journeys on with this recipe.

1506 U Street NW, Washington, DC 20009, (202) 588-7100, cakelove.com

SUSIE'S A PINK LADY LAYER CAKE

Makes two 9" X 2" Cake Layers, Enough for a 4-Layer Cake

FOR RASPBERRY PUREE:
12 ounces frozen raspberries
8 ounces granulated sugar

FOR ITALIAN MERINGUE BUTTERCREAM:
5 egg whites
1¼ cups, divided super fine granulated sugar
¼ cup water
12 ounces unsalted butter
Up to ½ cup raspberry puree
6½ ounces (13 tablespoons) unsalted butter (at room temperature)
14 ounces superfine granulated sugar
4 eggs

Special equipment: Candy thermometer, parchment paper

To prepare the puree: Combine the berries and sugar in a heavy bottom sauce pot and slowly bring to simmer. Continue to cook the berries at a very low rate for another 15 minutes. They should not burn. Strain through a tamis or other metal sieve; discard the seeds. Combine all of the pulp that gathered on the strained side of the sieve with the raspberry juices. Set aside to cool.

To prepare the buttercream: Combine 1 cup sugar and ¼ cup water in a heavy bottom sauce pot. Bring to 250°F (Chef Brown recommends using a Taylor® candy thermometer).

Meanwhile, bring the egg whites to stiff peak in a stand mixer fitted with the wire whip. Begin slowly, but increase the speed to high speed when the sugar syrup reaches 210°F.

Slowly pour in the ¼ cup sugar when the whites are at stiff peak. When the syrup reaches 250°F, slowly pour it into the meringue in a thin steady stream. The mixer should still be running while the syrup is being added. Continue to whip the meringue.

Cut the butter into small pieces while the meringue cools. After about 3 minutes, reduce to medium speed. After another 3 minutes, add the butter. Add the raspberry puree and mix on low speed until fully combined.

To prepare the cake: Preheat oven to 325°F. Cream butter in a stand mixer on medium speed. Change to low speed, add sugar, and mix for 3 minutes. Add eggs one at a time, turning off the mixer and scraping down the sides of the bowl after each egg is incorporated.

With the mixer on low speed, add the dry and wet ingredients alternately, starting and ending with dry. Turn off the mixer and scrape down the sides of the bowl again. Run the mixer on medium speed for 3–4 minutes to thoroughly combine all ingredients.

Line cake pans with parchment paper. Fill each cake pan ⅔ of the way and level with an offset spatula. Bake for 30–35 minutes or until golden brown across the top and a bamboo skewer poked into the center comes out clean.

Cool on a heat-resistant surface until room temperature. Use an offset spatula to release the cakes from the sides of the pans and invert onto a flat surface.

To assemble: Frost each layer of cake and stack atop one another.

DRY INGREDIENTS
(COMBINE WITH A WHISK AND SET ASIDE):
8 ounces all-purpose flour
2 ounces cocoa powder
2 ounces potato starch
1½ teaspoons baking powder
1 teaspoon salt

WET INGREDIENTS
(COMBINE AND SET ASIDE):
1 cup half & half
2 tablespoons brandy
2 teaspoons vanilla extract

CapMac Food Truck

http://capmacdc.com/
@CapMacDC

Brian Arnoff had a suspicion that if he built it they would come. What he didn't realize was that if he built it with wheels not only would they come but they would also line up for it. The "it," of course, is the ooey-gooey macaroni and cheese that he sells from his widely followed CapMac food truck. Arnoff, whose culinary journey took him to Florence, New York, and Boston before landing back in DC, always thought that someone should come up with a quick but high quality way to get a good bowl of pasta. Turns out he was that someone.

"I've always had this idea that I wanted to do a fast-food pasta concept," he says. "I always thought it was a shame that you couldn't get a good bowl of pasta quick. Then the whole food truck thing blew up and I thought the ideas fit together.

Clearly, Arnoff and his team—headed up by Chef Vicky Harris—have hit a comfort-food nerve. "On the grayest, darkest days, our lines are the longest," he tells.

The CapMac truck has a new team behind the wheel but still drives on bringing cheesy goodness to the streets of DC.

CLASSIC MAC

1 stick butter

½ cup flour

6 cups milk (warmed)

24 ounces white cheddar, shredded (preferably aged at least one year)

2 tablespoons Dijon mustard

1 tablespoon smoked paprika

½ cup roasted red peppers, pureed

Salt and pepper to taste

1 pound elbow macaroni

FOR THE TOPPING:

1 cup crushed Cheez-It crackers

1 cup shredded cheddar

Melt the butter in a large saucepan. Once completely melted, sprinkle in the flour and whisk to form a roux. Cook on high for about 2 minutes until the raw flour taste is just cooked out. Slowly pour warmed milk (you can warm the milk by pouring it in a measuring cup and microwaving it for 2–3 minutes) into the roux while whisking vigorously to avoid lumps. Cook the roux and milk mixture, or béchamel, for 3–5 minutes. Next add the shredded cheddar in two or three additions, slowly melting the cheese into the sauce. Finally, add the remaining ingredients: Dijon, paprika, red peppers, and salt and pepper to taste. The sauce should be thick and rich, with a bright orange color and a slight tang from the Dijon and red pepper puree.

Boil the elbows in salted water until al dente. Drain (but do not rinse), add to the cheese sauce, and cook 1–2 minutes more until the pasta and the sauce become one. Plate in deep bowls, sprinkling each with some shredded cheddar and a handful of crushed Cheez-It crackers.

Casa Luca

Tonno 'Briaco stands as a kind of a full circle dish for Casa Luca's Executive Chef Erin Clarke. She first made Chef Fabio Trabocchi's version of the drunken tuna more than a decade ago while assisting him with a cooking segment on a local television show. The recipe she helped prep, came from his book Cucina of Le Marche but all these years later the rustic dish still had not made an appearance on the menu of any of his restaurants. That is until Clarke took over the kitchen at Trabocchi's Casa Luca, his restaurant that focuses on dishes from Le Marche region where he grew up.

"I remember that this was one of his best recipes," Clarke tells. "But it was 12 years later, and we still hadn't had the opportunity to do it because everyone was doing fine dining. So when we were getting ready to open I said we have to include it. It was one of our first recipes."

The five-step dish works well as both an appetizer or as an entrée, Clarke explains but she prefers to serve it bruschetta style atop crusty bread. "The animal fat gives it nice complexity," says the former food educator who likes to ride her vintage bicycle to the downtown restaurant. "You could also use bacon fat instead of the lard."

Clarke, who trained in Paris, also adds bay leaves to this recipe, a popular ingredient at Casa Luca. "We buy our bay leaves from people who forage for them in the wild," says Clake who recommends storing them in the refrigerator. "They have strong flavor, which you want in this dish."

1099 New York Ave NW, Washington, DC 20001, (202) 525-1402, casalucadc.com

TONNO 'BRIACO (MARCHE STYLE DRUNKEN TUNA)

Serves 6

4 tablespoons (2 ounces)
    unsalted butter
4 anchovy fillets, packed in oil
3 tablespoons "manteca" or soft
    lard
2 ½ pounds tuna, cut into 6
    steaks approximately 1 inch
    thick
3 fresh bay leaves
2 cups dry Marsala
2 tablespoons finely chopped
    fresh Italian parsley
1 tablespoon drained and rinsed
    capers
2 tablespoons fresh lemon juice
Kosher salt and freshly ground
    white pepper
2 tablespoons extra virgin olive
    oil
6 slices of ½-inch thick crusty
    bread

Melt the butter in a small saucepan over low heat. Add the anchovies and mix well with a fork, pressing down on the anchovies until the mixture forms a paste At first it may look as if the butter won't be incorporated, but eventually it will. Remove from the heat and set aside.

Melt the manteca in a large skillet over medium-high heat. Once it is very hot, add the tuna and bay leaves. Sear the tuna for about 2 minutes per side, or until golden brown. Add the Marsala and bring to a boil. Reduce to a simmer, cover, and cook for 3-4 minutes, until the tuna is medium rare. Transfer the tuna to a platter and tent with aluminum foil to keep warm.

Remove and discard the bay leaves. Reduce the heat to low, keeping the liquid at a gentle simmer. Add the anchovy butter, parsley, capers and lemon juice, whisking or swirling the pan to blend the mixture into a smooth sauce. Season to taste with salt and pepper, remove from the heat, and set aside in a warm spot.

Heat the olive oil in a large saute pan over medium high heat. Add the bread and cook for approximately 1 minute per side, until just golden brown.

Arrange the bread in the middle of a serving dish or platter. Drizzle on some of the sauce, place the tuna on the bread, and spoon the remaining sauce over the fish.

At Casa Luca, this dish is served over a silky sweet turnip crema with mushroom funghetto.

Central Michel Richard

Philly has the cheesesteak. Chicago has deep-dish pizza. Buffalo its wings. And, some have started to say, DC has the burger. Over the last decade or so the burger seems to have taken its place as this city's unofficial dish. This is in no small part due to the creative takes on the classic sandwich that have been happening in the kitchens of renowned chefs like the late Michel Richard. Richard,'s lavish lobster burger preparation remains a perennial favorite among Central diners, often is held up as the gold standard of decadent burgers. The lobster offering, made of pure lobster meat, is one of several wildly popular non-beef burgers that has graced the Central menu. The others include an ahi tuna burger, a chicken and lemon burger, and a shrimp burger. But it's the lobster burger that owns the spotlight—to say nothing of the heftiest price tag.

The French-born Richard who died in 2016 opened Central as a chic yet casual follow-up to his flagship Georgetown restaurant Michel Richard Citronelle. Despite the $30 lobster burger, the Penn Quarter restaurant is more affordable than Citronelle and the dishes, a selection of American cuisine playfully infused with French flair, more approachable and familiar to most customers. (Think fried chicken, short ribs, and banana splits.) The burger menu is not the only place the chef re-imagines the norm. Richard's recipe for a homemade version of the Kit Kat bar still wows customers on a daily basis and joins the lobster burger as one of the restaurant's most talked about dishes.

1001 Pennsylvania Avenue NW, Washington, DC 20004, (202) 626-0015, centralmichelrichard.com

LOBSTER BURGER

Makes 4 Burgers

FOR THE TOMATOES:

4 slices tomato, ½-inch thick
½ teaspoon granulated sugar
Fine sea salt and freshly ground
  black pepper
1 teaspoon extra-virgin olive oil
1 sprig fresh thyme leaves
1 garlic clove, peeled and thinly
  sliced

FOR THE LOBSTER BURGERS:

2 (2-pound) lobsters
Fine sea salt and freshly ground
  black pepper
¼ cup mayonnaise, plus extra for
  chip assembly
½ teaspoon grated fresh ginger
1 tablespoon (½ ounce) unsalted
  butter, preferably clarified
  butter
1 tablespoon plus 1 teaspoon
  olive oil
4 hamburger buns, homemade or
  store-bought
16 wafer-thin potato chips
1 cup mâche

To prepare the tomatoes: Preheat the oven to 225°F. Line a baking sheet with a Silpat or parchment paper. Place the tomato slices on the lined pan. Sprinkle with a light dusting of sugar, salt, and pepper, then drizzle lightly with olive oil. Top with the thyme leaves and garlic slices. Place in the oven for 30 minutes to 1 hour to dry slightly and concentrate the flavor.

Cool the tomatoes on the pan, then cover and refrigerate for up to a day. Bring to room temperature before using.

To prepare the lobster burgers: Place enough water to cover the lobsters in a large stockpot and bring to a boil. Fill one or two large bowls (to hold the lobsters) with ice water. Place the lobsters in the boiling water for 2 minutes. Remove the lobsters from the pot and place in the ice water until cold. Remove and drain thoroughly.

Working over a bowl, break the lobsters apart and reserve any juices.

To remove the meat, grasp the tail, twist, and pull to detach it from each lobster. Twist off the claws. Discard the bodies or reserve for stock or another use. Twist to separate the knuckles from the claws. Use kitchen shears to cut through the shell on the smooth side of the knuckles, and pull out the meat. Using scissors, cut down the center of the underside of each tail. Pull the shell back and remove the meat. Cut the tail meat lengthwise in half. Remove and discard the vein that runs along the top of the tail. Cut the tail meat and knuckle meat into ½- to ¾-inch pieces and place in a small bowl.

Pull down on the small claw pincers to loosen them and then pull them away from the claws. Crack the wide section of claw shell with the back of a chef's knife and pull apart to remove the meat. Cut the claw meat into 2-inch pieces, and place in the bowl of a small food processor. Blend on high speed to a paste. Season with salt and pepper, add to the chopped lobster meat, and combine with a rubber spatula.

Divide the lobster into 4 equal parts and form each into a burger just about the size of the buns. Place on a plate and cover with plastic wrap. Refrigerate for 2 to 3 hours to firm.

Combine the mayonnaise and grated ginger in a small bowl. Cover and refrigerate until ready to use.

Preheat the oven to 350°F. If you have a second oven, preheat the broiler.

In a large ovenproof nonstick skillet, melt the butter with 1 tablespoon of the olive oil over medium heat. Place the burger in the pan and cook on the first side for 1 to 2 minutes. Flip and cook on the second side for another 2 minutes. Flip again and cook for another minute. Transfer to the oven and bake for 4 minutes, or until warm in the center. To check, insert the tip of a small paring knife into the center of a patty, and then touch the knife tip. If it is warm, the burgers are ready.

To serve: Split buns in half, place on a baking sheet, and lightly toast under the broiler. Or, if you do not have two ovens, turn the broiler on once the burgers are removed, and toast the buns.

Spread about half of the ginger mayonnaise on the bun halves. Using the remaining mayonnaise as "glue," make four stacks of four potato chips each. In a small bowl, toss the mâche with the remaining teaspoon of oil.

Place the lobster burgers on the bottom halves of the buns. Top each with a slice of roasted tomato, a stack of layered chips, and about ¼ cup of mâche.

Chef's note: The lobster is initially undercooked. It is placed in boiling water long enough to loosen the meat from the shell to make removing it easier. Then the lobster is cooked again after the burgers are formed.

Co Co. Sala

Santosh Tiptur didn't have his first taste of french toast until he was nineteen years old. And, if you pardon the cliché, it was love at first bite.

The Bangalore-born chef grew up eating traditional Indian breakfast foods and did not happen upon the classic American favorite until he started working in the kitchens of hotels in his hometown. "As an adult I fell in love with french toast," says Tiptur, who has played around with different variations of the dish throughout his career. The decadent French Toast S'mores he created for Co Co. Sala are a personal and customer favorite.

Although the dish has many components, eleven to be exact, when it's made at the restaurant, the chef reassures me that it's not a hard one to replicate at home. The milk chocolate mousse can be made up to a day in advance and, while Tiptur uses house-made marshmallows and cinnamon brioche, store-bought versions also can do the job. Be it store-bought or house-made, the chef does recommend brioche over other breads for his chocolate-and-marshmallow-laden french toast. Brioche adds a texture and fluffiness to the end product and is easy to work with in this particular recipe. "Brioche is firmer when it's cold," explains Tiptur who worked as the executive pastry chef at the Ritz-Carlton, San Juan, and on cruise lines for twelve years before coming to Washington. "But when you warm it up it's as soft as cotton."

The Co Co. Sala chef traces his passion for working with food and putting flavors together back to India. As a young child he loved helping his mother cook and fondly remembers going to the market about twice a week to seek out the best vegetables and other ingredients for her. After 10 years, Co Co. Sala closed in February 2018, but the memories of the food here live on.

FRENCH TOAST S'MORES

Serves 8

MILK CHOCOLATE MOUSSE:

1¼ cups heavy cream

⅔ cup egg yolk

⅔ cup sugar

2 cups milk chocolate

1 cup heavy cream

1 teaspoon unflavored gelatin
     dissolved in ¼ cup cold water

2 tablespoons Kahlua

BANANA FOSTER:

⅔ cup water

1 cup sugar

1 vanilla bean pods

1 cinnamon stick

⅔ cup cream

¼ cup butter

⅔ cup banana liquor

¼ cup rum

**CHOCOLATE GANACHE (FOR
     SAUCE):**

½ cup chocolate, dark

⅔ cup heavy cream

1 tablespoon glucose

1 tablespoon butter, unsalted

To prepare the mousse: Start by whipping 1¼ cups of cream until soft peaks form.

Place the chocolate in a mixing bowl. Heat the additional 1 cup of cream and pour over the milk chocolate. Whisk together until well combined to create a ganache.

In a double boiler, whip the yolks and sugar until the sugar is slightly dissolved and then transfer contents to another mixing bowl. Whip until the volume has tripled. Add the yolks one at a time. Then fold in the ganache, the melted gelatin, the whipped cream, and finally the Kahlua, into the yolk mixture. Cover and refrigerate overnight.

VANILLA-CINNAMON SUGAR:

½ vanilla bean
½ cup refined sugar
¼ teaspoon cinnamon, ground

EGG BATTER FOR DIPPING THE
FRENCH TOAST:

1 cup milk
¼ cup heavy cream
¼ cup sugar
1 tablespoon vanilla extract
4 large eggs
½ vanilla bean pod

16 slices of cinnamon brioche or
    cinnamon bread
32 jet puffed marshmallows
8 dark chocolate truffle cut in
    quarters
16 graham cracker cookies
4 ripe bananas cut in ½-inch
    slices

To prepare the banana foster: Place the water, sugar, vanilla bean, and cinnamon stick in a heavy bottom pot and cook the sugar until it starts to turn a light amber color. When this happens the sugar will begin to cook quickly. Soon you will notice that the mixture will turn a dark amber color. When this happens that means it has reached caramel stage.

Remove it from the heat once you have determined that the mixture has reached the caramel stage. Add the cream and butter and whisk thoroughly. Add the banana liquor and rum and mix well. Set aside.

To prepare the chocolate ganache: First place the chocolate in a medium bowl. Heat the heavy cream and glucose in a pan over medium heat. Bring to a boil and pour over the chocolate. Let sit until it starts melting. Mix with a whisk until well combined. Set aside.

To prepare the cinnamon sugar: Cut the vanilla bean lengthwise. Scrape the pulp out from inside of the bean and mix it with sugar and ground cinnamon. Mix well and put it aside for later use.

To prepare the batter: Heat the milk, cream, and sugar over a low heat until the sugar crystals are dissolved. Add the vanilla extract and the eggs. Scrape the vanilla bean into mixture and mix well.

To assemble and serve the final dish: Slice the bread in ½-inch slices. Spread the chocolate ganache on one slice. Place 4 toasted marshmallows, one chocolate truffle cut in quarters, and one graham cracker cookie square on top.

Take another slice and spread the chocolate ganache and make a sandwich with the slice, which is topped with the toasted marshmallow, graham cracker cookie, and chocolate truffle. Repeat this process with rest of the bread.

Dip the s'mores sandwiches you have just created into the French toast egg batter, making sure both the sides are not over soaked.

Heat a non-stick pan on the stove over a medium flame. Once a sandwich is coated with the batter, place it in the heated pan. Add a few drops of melted butter to the pan and cook until golden brown on each side.

Once all the bread is cooked, place the banana foster caramel in medium pan over a medium heat. Add in the bananas and toss until well coated. Transfer into a small serving dish.

Coat the French toast on all sides with the cinnamon sugar mixture and then cut the French toast diagonally. Artfully arrange the slices on a large platter. Serve with the chocolate mousse and the banana foster on the side.

Comet Ping Pong

From the tabletops to the tomatoes, James Alefantis's touch is everywhere at Comet Ping Pong.

Each year Alefantis and his team head out to Shippensburg, Pennsylvania, for a pilgrimage of the sauce. First stop, the Toigo Orchard, a family-owned farm. There they help harvest the ten tons (yes, tons) of organic tomatoes the farm grows each year just for the restaurant. After a very long day of picking, the tomatoes are loaded onto a truck and then driven off to Punxsutawny, Pennsylvania, home of the clairvoyant groundhog and one of the area's last canneries where Comet makes all of its pizza sauce for the coming year. There, hundreds of pounds of tomatoes get peeled, stewed, seasoned, and stored, but not before Alefantis tastes and refines the batches coming through, making tweaks and adjustments along the way until the red sauce is perfect and ready to be jarred. Finally, the finished product gets loaded onto the truck for the journey home to Connecticut Avenue. Once there, the sauce is unpacked and stored below ground in the basement space that runs below the restaurant.

Alefantis's involvement with the final product at Comet does not end with the tomatoes. He also poured the cement for the pizza oven, designed the industrial-age-meets-slice space, and even hauled and refinished reclaimed wood to create the distressed benches attached to the table tennis–like tables in the dining room. Many a night he makes the from-scratch rustic pizzas that come from Comet's busy kitchen and he is responsible for dreaming up the concept of a neighborhood pizza parlor with table tennis in the back and indie bands late at night. It is this kind of personal touch that has allowed Comet to distinguish itself on the restaurant scene and it's his busy kitchen that has helped take DC out of the pizza dead zone.

It's also what makes a true neighborhood gem, with kids and families and hipsters often eating alongside one another.

5037 Connecticut Avenue NW, Washington, DC 20008, (202) 364-0404, cometpingpong.com

THE SMOKY PIZZA
Makes 4–6 Pizzas

FOR THE PIZZA DOUGH:
7 to 8 cups organic white flour
2½ cups water
½ ounce active yeast
Pinch of salt

FOR THE RED PIE:
Comet Pizza Sauce made from
    Toigo tomatoes or seasoned
    pureed canned tomatoes
Mix of low-moisture mozzarella
    and fresh Blue Ridge Dairy
    mozzarella

FOR THE SMOKY PIE:
Garlic oil
Melted onions
Smoked and fresh mozzarella
Smoked bacon
Smoked mushrooms

Make the pizza dough: Place all ingredients in electric mixer. With the paddle, mix until the dough comes together (about 3 minutes). Then mix on a slower setting for an additional 7-8 minutes. Let dough stand at room temperature for 1 hour. Cut the dough into 4 or 6 pieces and shape into balls.

Place the dough balls in the refrigerator for an additional 3–4 hours. Be sure to take the dough out of refrigerator about 20 minutes prior to baking so it can cool down to room temperature before shaping.

To prepare the pizzas: If using a home oven, place the pizza stone in the oven and preheat on bake for at least 3 hours at your oven's highest listed temperature (usually 500°F).

Sprinkle a wooden pizza peel with semolina flour. If you don't have a pizza peel you can use a floured wooden cutting board or cookie sheet.

Hand-stretch the dough into something looking like a pizza (don't worry about it being exactly round).

Place on peel then ladle on some Comet Pizza Sauce and cheese mix for the Red Pie. Or top with any delicious toppings.

Slide pizzas onto stone and cook 5–6 minutes, or until crust is puffy and charred in places and the cheese has fully melted. Use the peel (or a large spatula) to quickly slide under the pizza and remove it from the oven.

For the famous Smoky Pizza, top the dough in this order: Garlic oil, melted onions, low-moisture mozzarella, smoked mozzarella, smoked bacon, and smoked mushrooms.

Enjoy with a beer, right before or after playing PING PONG!

DGS Delicatessen

DGS Delicatessen tells many stories at once. The story of how a pair of third-generation Washingtonians brought good deli to DC. The story of the renaissance of an immigrant cuisine. And, the personal Jewish American story of owners and cousins Nick Wiseman and David Wiseman – their family's narrative that helped guide them toward restaurant ownership.

During the early part of the 20th Century, mom-and-pop grocers lined the streets of DC. Jews who had fled persecution in Eastern Europe and Russia owned many of these small independent markets. Typically the owners and their families lived above the store, worked long hours, and faced challenges just as many immigrant groups did and still do when they come to this country.

One massive hurdle facing these shopkeepers was keeping the shelves stocked despite the discrimination they faced from wholesalers who did not want to sell to them, Jewish immigrants and refugees. In order to survive, the owners joined together to form District Grocery Stores, or DGS, a buying cooperative that leveraged the power of the many independent stores linked together as one. At its peak, there were approximately 300 member stores throughout DC, including the one owned by Nick and David's grandfather, Leon Wiseman.

"On the wall when you walk in door on right, that's the family store," Nick says of the blown up black-and-white photo of Leon's DGS that once sat on 16th Street. Other similar photos of other DGS stores and families dot the walls of the modern deli. A few of the old photos are even printed on old commercial-sized baking sheets. The images and the food remind the owners and customers of the broader picture both literally and figuratively.

"The premise of DGS is the story of our family coming to DC and the large narrative of the immigrant story," Nick says. "Our grandfather had to travel on a friend's papers to get into US. He desperately wanted to be American. He was chasing the American dream. It's the same story being told today. The immigrant experience of DGS is becoming more relevant than ever."

While the inspiration came from their family's journey, they had to reach back a bit further when it came time to putting together a menu. "We spent more meals eating in Chinese restaurants together than in delicatessens," Nick says.

Using their culinary training, kitchen skills, and Jewish food pride, the cousins began studying the origins, methods, and art behind brining, smoking, pickling, curing, and the like. "A lot of this food is just time," he says. "In general it takes time to make things taste better. If you look at history you generally see poor people taking lesser quality food [and using these methods] to make last longer or taste better."

The old world flavors and techniques along with freshly sourced ingredients elevate the deli food to a modern platform without a trace of lesser quality anything in site. (The team makes the short walk every Sunday to the Dupont Circle farmer's market and wheels down boxes and boxes of fresh produce.) The Dupont Circle delicatessen offers its customers choices of many new takes on old favorites like matzo ball soup, smoked whitefish, smoked salmon, potato latkes, chopped liver, stuffed cabbage, and house-made pastrami and corned beef. Everything from the pickles to pastrami is made in house except the bread, which is brought in and then double baked on site. There even is a sandwich named for the grandfather who helped inspire it all: The Leon is smoked turkey, chopped liver, coleslaw, and Russian dressing on double baked rye. An overstuffed sandwich tribute to the man who the pair refer to as "our scrappy urban pioneer."

1317 Connecticut Ave NW, Washington, DC 20036, (202) 293-4400, dgsdelicatessen.com

BRINE AND SCHNITZEL

1 cup water
1 cup whole buttermilk
¼ cup kosher salt
3 cloves garlic, crushed
2 bay leaves
3 sprigs fresh oregano, plus a
    few leaves for garnish
1 teaspoon deli mustard
Four 7-ounce boneless, skinless
    chicken thighs (fat trimmed
    off, if desired)

BREAD CRUMB MIXTURE
2 cups flour
2 large eggs, lightly beaten
2 cups fresh rye bread crumbs
1 teaspoon onion powder
1 teaspoon garlic powder
¼ cup canola oil

For the brine and schnitzel: Combine the water and buttermilk in a medium saucepan over medium heat. Add the salt, stirring until it has dissolved. Transfer the mixture to a deep container; once it has cooled, add the garlic, bay leaves, oregano and deli mustard.

Working with one at a time, place the chicken thighs between pieces of plastic wrap. Pound them evenly thin, discard the wrap, then add the thighs to the brine, making sure they are submerged. Cover and refrigerate for at least 4 hours.

When you're ready to fry the schnitzel, discard the marinade and pat the chicken thighs dry with paper towels.

Spread one cup of the flour in a shallow bowl, and pour the beaten eggs into a second bowl. Whisk together the remaining cup of flour, the fresh rye bread crumbs, the onion powder and garlic powder in a wide, shallow bowl. Layer paper towels under a wire rack.

Coat each chicken thigh in the following order: flour, then egg, then bread crumb mixture, making sure the last coating completely covers the meat. If you have time, let the coated pieces of chicken sit on the rack for 5 minutes; this will help the coating remain on the schnitzel as it cooks.

Heat the oil in a medium skillet over medium heat. Cook the schnitzels one at a time for a total of 3 minutes, until golden brown on both sides and cooked through. Transfer to the rack to drain.

SMOKED HONEY DRESSING
1 cup cider vinegar
1½ cups canola oil
¼ cup smoked honey
2 tablespoons black pepper
1 tablespoon kosher salt

PICKLED MUSTARD SEEDS
1 cup yellow mustard seeds
1½ cups water
1½ cups white rice vinegar
½ cup sugar
1 tablespoon kosher salt

CAULIFLOWER PUREE
2 tablespoons butter
1 large sweet onion, thinly sliced
1 head cauliflower, trimmed and
    cut into florets
2 cups water
2 bay leaves
2 tablespoons kosher salt

Mix together all ingredients and slowly emulsify oil to make dressing

Combine mustard seeds, water, vinegar, sugar, and salt in a saucepan and bring to a simmer over low heat for 45 minutes to an hour

In a large pan, cook onion in butter over medium heat until they begin to caramelize. Add cauliflower and cook until rich golden color, ~15 minutes. Add torn bay leaves, water and salt. Cook over low heat for 30 minutes. Remove bay leaves and puree until smooth and creamy.

MAZEL TOV COCKTAIL

Serves 1

¼ ounce lavender syrup (recipe below)
1 ounce Averell Damson plum gin liqueur, or quality sloe gin
Splash of fresh lemon juice
4 ounces Champagne or sparkling wine

LAVENDER SYRUP
2 ounces dried lavender buds
2 cups water
1½ cup sugar

To make the lavender syrup: Pour two cups of water in a saucepan and soak lavender buds for 5 minutes. Add sugar, and then bring to a simmer for 7 minutes over medium heat, stirring occasionally. Cool and strain. Syrup will last for 3 to 4 weeks in the refrigerator.

When you're ready to serve, pour lavender syrup, gin, and lemon in a mixing glass over ice, stir briefly, and strain into Champagne flute. Top with chilled Champagne and serve.

A Few Tricks of the Trade from James

"Garlic oil is a great thing to have on hand for many things and it keeps for a week or more (or freeze). The oil imparts the deliciousness of garlic while removing its bitterness or pungency. Simply submerge lots of sliced garlic in a good olive oil and very gently simmer until the garlic gets soft. Spoon oil and the soft garlic onto anything."

"Melted onions are also great to have around or freeze for onion pizzas or tarts or quick pasta sauces, etc. Simply slice many fresh white onions and cook in a large pan with lots of olive oil. Cook the onions VERY slowly and DO NOT brown. Add lots of fresh thyme while cooking and take the onions off the heat after they have released much of their juices and are soft."

"Buy a great smoked bacon (we use a brand called Old Smokehouse) and slice and bake it until it just starts to crisp."

"For the smoked mushrooms we slice up cremini (button) mushrooms and smoke them over our wood grill and then sauté with whole garlic cloves and olive oil. If you don't have a smoker they will be great just sautéed."

"We sometimes smoke our own mozzarella but a great local cheese is Blue Ridge Dairy smoked mozzarella."

District Commons

It sounds like a throwaway to say that something is so good you can put it on almost anything, but it's the honest truth when it comes to the Beer Mustard Butter at District Commons. The stuff truly holds its own on sandwiches, cornbread, veggies, meats, and breads, and I must admit that I have seen at least two people eat the stuff off a spoon at this Foggy Bottom restaurant, which sits right on Washington Circle. In house, Beer Mustard Butter comes served with a warm pretzel baguette.. The combination makes for a can't-take-just-one-bite experience and it pairs well with one of the many American beer offerings at the light-filled, modern-day, tavern-type eatery. If you want an earworm with your brew, order from the "99 Beers on the Wall" wall, but please keep the singing to yourself or you might wind up dining alone.

The greatest time commitment with this recipe comes from the need to refrigerate the mustard seeds, vinegar, and beer overnight, which means it's not something you can just whip up an hour before company comes over or during the pre-game show. But if you remember to do the first step the day before, the rest of the prep goes relatively quickly and is pretty straightforward. As with anything, the better the quality of the ingredients (especially when it comes to the butter, dark beer, honey, and mustard seeds), the better the final product. This recipe is intended for a large crowd, think Super Bowl party or family reunion, but leftovers freeze well.

2200 Pennsylvania Avenue NW, Washington, DC 20037, (202) 587-8277, districtcommonsdc.com

BEER MUSTARD BUTTER

Yields 1 Quart

¼ cup black mustard seeds
¼ cup yellow mustard seeds
¾ cup malt vinegar
1⅓ cups dark beer
1 cup honey
¼ cup dark brown sugar
1 tablespoon salt
1 tablespoon allspice
1¼ teaspoons turmeric
½ cup dry mustard
3 cups butter, unsalted and
softened

Combine the mustard seeds and vinegar with ¾ of the beer and refrigerate overnight. In a saucepan combine remaining beer with honey, brown sugar, salt, allspice, and turmeric and bring to a boil. Remove from heat and allow to cool completely. Once cool, transfer to blender. Add ground mustard and soaked mustard seeds with their liquids. Puree in blender until smooth.

Separate ½ cup of the mustard mixture and add to 3 cups of softened butter. Whip together until evenly mixed and season to taste with salt. Repeat with remaining mixture of mustard (combining 1 part mixture to 6 parts butter) or store in refrigerator for future use. Serve with pretzel baguette or other breads.

Equinox

Theirs is a romance of the food fairy-tale sort. Sous chef meets sales rep, sous chef and sales rep fall in love, sous chef and sales rep get married and open restaurants as they ride off into the sunset. OK, it might not be coming to a theater near you anytime soon, but it is more or less the story of how Equinox co-owners Ellen Kassoff Gray and Todd Gray met once upon a time. "I was a food sales rep and he was a sous chef," she tells. "He was trying to pick up his sales rep."

Fast-forward a bunch of years to 1995 and the pair, both of whom started working in restaurants as teenagers, opened Equinox, their first professional undertaking together. "We came up with the idea just by looking at what was around us naturally," Ellen recalls. "Food at that time had gotten so far away from seasonal and local focus. Now, of course, it's what's normal and expected."

On Sundays the couple offers a full vegan brunch, a concept close to their hearts. The couple embraces "domestic veganism" at home, which means they are omnivores outside of the house but cook without animal products of any kind at home. "The mission of the cafe is to have a balance of vegan, vegetarian, and traditional foods in a public space such as a gallery," says Ellen, who does the majority of the cooking at home. "The clientele really appreciates it. Whether you're a carnivore or full-fledged vegan, you should at least try to be plant-based one or two days a week. It's a great way to live and it's the ultimate in conservation."

818 Connecticut Avenue NW, Washington, DC 20006, (202) 331-8118, equinoxrestaurant.com

RISOTTO FRITTERS

Makes 36

FOR THE FRITTERS:

¼ cup olive oil

1 cup minced yellow onion

3 cups Arborio rice

1 cup white wine

6 cups vegetable broth

Water as needed

2 tablespoons butter

1 cup finely grated parmesan cheese

½ teaspoon salt

½ teaspoon pepper

Canola oil for frying

FOR THE BREAD CRUMBS:

3 cups panko bread crumbs

2 cups flour

4 eggs beaten for wash

Heat a 4-quart saucepan on medium heat. Add oil and onions and cook for 3 minutes. Add Arborio rice and "toast" for 1 minute. Add white wine and reduce until dry. Add hot vegetable broth ⅓ cup at a time. Stir the rice and let it absorb the broth between additions. Cook rice for 14–16 minutes or until al dente. If broth runs out before rice is cooked, continue cooking with additions of water. Remove from heat and stir in butter, Parmesan, and season with salt and pepper. Pour risotto onto a sheet pan and cool in fridge. While the risotto is cooling, take the panko bread crumbs and run them through a food processor. This will help make for a smooth, crispy finish when the fritters are fried.

When the risotto is completely chilled, form walnut-sized balls using your hands. Take the risotto balls and one a time roll them in the flour, then the beaten egg, and finally in the bread crumbs that have been run through the processor. Repeat with each risotto ball and make sure to keep to this order—flour, egg, bread crumbs. Once completed, keep the fritters cold until you are ready to fry them.

Before serving, fry the risotto balls in canola oil until golden brown on all sides.

Estadio

Some people like to gaze for hours into the night sky. Others get their muse on by watching the waves break against the shoreline. For Chef Haidar Karoum, inspiration often appears from watching other chefs practice their craft. One of his favorite spots to spend a day in New York was a restaurant with a kitchen bar where he could observe other chefs carefully prepare each order as it came in. "I would go there and literally sit for hours and hours," says Karoum. "When it came time to open, we thought, why can't we do that here?"

Thankfully they did. The counter seating perched above a kitchen at the 14th Street tapas restaurant now also offers kitchen fans and casual observers seating where they, too, can observe the art of cooking as they order from the menu of small plates and cocktails. For a few weeks in the spring, ramps become a popular player on that open stage. A scallion-like vegetable often described as having the flavor of both garlic and onion, ramps play a key role in the chef's divine Ramps with Smoky Romesco & Manchego Cheese dish at Estadio, which not coincidentally is the Spanish word for stadium.

Karoum derived his inspiration for the dish from the Spanish wild onion calçot, another spring onion with a very short and anticipated season. In Spain celebrations called calçotada have grown up around the vegetable. The tender calçots are charred over an open flame and then dipped in romesco sauce. Estadio's version pays homage to this tradition and captures its smoky taste. When ramps, or calçot for that matter, are not available, leeks or scallions make for good substitutions. A glass of red wine with the dish, be it one using calçots, ramps, or scallions, is not mandatory but highly encouraged.

Chef Haidar Karoum has left the Estadio kitchen but happily ramp season—and this recipe—is forever.

1520 14th Street NW, Washington, DC 20005. (202) 319-1404, estadio-dc.com

RAMPS WITH SMOKY ROMESCO & MANCHEGO CHEESE

Serves 6 to 8

FOR THE ROMESCO SAUCE:

¼ white onion, peeled and cut in chunks

¼ whole jalapeño

1 medium red bell peppers, whole

1 tomatoes, whole

¼ cup olive oil, plus ¼ tablespoon for vegetables

¼ cup almonds, blanched and peeled

¼ cup toasted, cubed bread

1 clove garlic

¼ cup water

½ tablespoon sherry vinegar

⅛ teaspoon pimenton (smoked Spanish paprika)

½ teaspoon salt, or more to taste

1 bunch ramps or scallions, washed, rinsed, and roots trimmed

½ tablespoon olive oil

Salt and pepper to taste

¼ cup romesco sauce (recipe below)

¼ cup grated Manchego cheese

To prepare the romesco sauce: Set a grill or broiler to high. In a medium bowl, toss together the onions, jalapeño, red peppers, and tomatoes in ¼ cup oil and salt. Grill, turning occasionally, until they're charred and lightly sweating juice. If broiling, lay out vegetables on a foil-lined baking sheet.

Put all the grilled vegetables in a large bowl and cover with plastic wrap. Let cool for 10–15 minutes. Remove the seeds from the jalapeño and bell peppers and peel the peppers. Leave everything else whole.

While the vegetables are cooling, heat a pan over medium-low heat and add ¼ tablespoon of olive oil. Fry the blanched almonds, cubed bread, and garlic. Cook until golden, about 4 minutes. Remove the toasted ingredients from the oil. Save the oil.

Place the vegetables with their accumulated juices into a blender along with the toasted bread, almonds, garlic, and ¼ cup of water. Blend until combined, and then add the vinegar, pimenton, and ½ teaspoon salt. Blend again while slowly adding the saved olive oil. Taste and adjust seasoning. Set aside to cool to room temperature.

To finish: Heat a grill or broiler to high. Toss ramps with the olive oil, salt, and pepper. Grill about 1 minute per side, until lightly charred. Place ramps on a plate. Top with romesco sauce and Manchego cheese.

Fiola

Growing up in Italy Chef Fabio Trabocchi almost never set foot in a supermarket. Instead he spent Saturdays going from farm to farm with his father to get what they needed for the week. The best eggs came from one farm, the best chickens from another, the best tomatoes from yet another. After the best of everything was purchased, the cooking began. "I guess I am one of the last of my generation of chefs to have one foot in that past," Trabocchi says. "Even our water came from a natural source."

"When I woke up on Sunday mornings, there always was tomato sauce on the fire," recalls Trabocchi, the son of a third-generation farmer who had a passion for cooking. "Maybe there would be a duck roasting or my father would be carving a rabbit. Or maybe I'd be going down to a garden in front of our house to collect artichokes."

Vivid memories of taste, sight, and smell continue to guide him and the way he approaches his craft. At the Michelin-starred Fiola, Trabocchi almost exclusively stocks his kitchen from independent farmers. "The chef attributes his attitude toward experimenting with food to his Italian roots." "The first and most important thing to keep in mind is to keep it simple and don't overthink it," he says of this meatball recipe. "If you want a bit more ground pork, add it. If you want some more ground bacon, add that. If you want an extra handful of cheese, that's OK too. Trust me, this behavior is as Italian as could be. As long as the proportions are about the same it will turn out in the end. The Italians don't codify things. In Italy even the same thing with the same name is different from home to home, from community to community, from village to village. So don't be afraid to make the recipe your own."

601 Pennsylvania Ave NW, Washington, DC 20004, (202) 628-2888, fioladc.com

MEATBALLS

Serves 8

3 garlic cloves, peeled
1 cup plus 3 tablespoons
    extra-virgin olive oil
3 cups white bread, cubed
3 cups heavy cream
1 pound ground beef
1 pound ground veal
½ pound ground pork
6 egg yolks
2 cups grated pecorino Romano
    cheese
6 tablespoons chopped Italian
    parsley
Salt and pepper
1 cup canola oil for sautéing the
    meatballs

Cook the garlic cloves over low heat in a small saucepan with 3 tablespoons of extra-virgin olive oil until soft and translucent. Set aside to cool down and mash the cloves with a back of a spoon. In a bowl, soak the bread in the cream until completely soaked. Leave time to allow the bread to fully absorb the cream. Place all the ingredients (except canola oil) in a bowl, including the garlic with oil and the soaked bread. Mix well and let it rest in the refrigerator for about 30 minutes.

Form the meat mixture into golf ball-sized balls. Heat canola oil in large sauté pan. Working in small batches, sauté the meatballs until golden brown on all sides and cooked through.

As rule of thumb, most ground meats will produce a good meatball.

Firefly

Warm memories and nostalgia serve as the main ingredients for Chef Daniel "Danny" Bortnick's popular Chicken Matzoh Ball Soup. Chef Danny no longer works in the kitchen at Firefly, but he is still involved as Vice President of Restaurant Concept Development for Kimpton Hotels and Restaurants. Memory, nostalgia, and a hint of dill, that is. So when Bortnick helped craft the menu for Firefly around the idea of classic American comfort foods done anew, his mom's matzoh ball soup immediately came to mind. A traditional choice for a Jewish kitchen, but a rather unconventional one for a mainstream restaurant of Firefly's caliber. "You don't ever really walk into a good restaurant and see matzoh ball soup on the menu," explains Bortnick, who remembers eating the steamy soup at holiday meals and Friday-night family dinners when he was growing up in Rockville. "But I ultimately decided that I wanted to create a menu that had a connection to me."

Danny advises only cooking the chicken soup—any chicken stock—for forty-five minutes after it comes to a boil, a tip he learned from a Chinese chef that he likes to pass on to others. "After forty-five minutes you've got all the flavor you are going to get," he says.

While the flavorful soup and the light and fluffy matzoh balls are a shout-out to his mom, the dill is an homage to the now-defunct Celebrity Delly, a suburban Maryland fixture when Bortnick was growing up where the matzoh balls were made with fresh chopped dill.

1310 New Hampshire Avenue NW, Washington, DC 20036, (202) 861-1310, firefly-dc.com

CHICKEN MATZOH BALL SOUP

Makes About 20 Portions

FOR THE SOUP:

4 organic chicken carcasses

4 cups chopped yellow onion

1 cup chopped celery

6 garlic cloves, peeled and cut
    in half

8 sprigs thyme

8 sprigs parsley

1 bay leaf

2 cups chopped carrots, placed
    in a cheesecloth bag

Salt and pepper to taste

4 quarts cold water

FOR THE MATZOH BALLS:

16 large organic eggs

1 cup reserved chicken fat,
    melted

1 cup seltzer water

2 tablespoons salt

1 tablespoon pepper

½ cup fresh dill, chopped

4 cups matzoh meal

Special equipment: A 2-ounce ice cream scoop to make the matzoh balls, although you can use your hands, too.

To prepare the soup: Place all the soup ingredients (chicken carcasses, onion, celery, garlic cloves, thyme, parsley, bay leaf, carrots, salt, pepper, and water) in a pot and bring to a boil. Reduce to a simmer and cook 45 minutes (but no more than that!). Skim fat off the top of the soup and reserve for matzoh balls. Strain broth through a sieve and adjust seasoning. Remove the carrots from the cheesecloth and pass through a food mill and then add them back to the soup.

To prepare the matzoh balls: Beat the eggs. Add chicken fat, seltzer water, salt, pepper, and the dill. Mix thoroughly. Add matzoh meal and mix well. Refrigerate for 1 hour. Bring a pot of salted water to a boil. With a 2-ounce ice cream scoop, form balls and drop into water. Simmer, covered, for 45 minutes and then shock in ice water. When cool, store the matzoh balls in Ziploc bags and date them for future reference. Matzoh balls can keep for about a week in the refrigerator and can also be frozen. Reheat the matzoh balls in the soup.

Founnding Farmers

Chef Joe Goetze remembers the moment he knew he wanted to be a chef. It was 1987. He was making $6.60 an hour working in the kitchen at the Hyatt Regency in Greenwich, Connecticut. Each morning, the space would fill up with the sounds of the staff talking about what they did last night, complaining about shifts or bickering over things that happened earlier in the week. It was crowded and noisy. Very noisy. That is, until the chef walked in. At that moment the fighting and joking stopped. It got quiet. Very quiet. So quiet you could hear a silicon quarter teaspoon drop. "I want to be that guy," Goetze remembers thinking that morning. He was in high school at the time.

It took time and a lot of hard work, but now he is that guy. Today Goetze serves as vice president of culinary development and managing partner of bakery operations for the Farmers Restaurant Group. He drives the menu and food decisions at the popular Founding Famers restaurants, built around the farm-to-table concept coupled with the American cooking tradition, and he works to keep the concept fresh and fluid. Still, the Culinary Institute of America graduate credits that first hotel job as an important layer of the foundation on which he has built his successful culinary career. At the hotel he did everything from banquet prep to coffee service to butchery, which was common practice at hotels at the time.

Founding Famers was also formed on a holistic approach, albeit a decidedly different one. The downtown restaurant, as well as its Potomac location, prides itself on sourcing natural and organic ingredients with a light carbon footprint whenever possible. It also is committed to passing along to customers the origins of the foods it uses in its kitchen. The fried green tomatoes and beignets are just two tasty examples of the dishes that come out of this approach. Goetze stresses the importance of keeping your oil clean during the frying process and notes that you can use the batter for the fried green tomatoes for just about anything. For the beignets he recommends adding a sprinkle of salt and filling them with ice cream or really anything sweet that you would put in a pie crust. However you decide to dress up the dishes, the chef encourages you to put your own spin on them. "Make the recipe once to get to know the recipe and then start to cook it to your own style," he says. "Then the recipe becomes your recipe."

1924 Pennsylvania Avenue NW, Washington, DC 20006, (202) 822-8783
wearefoundingfarmers.com

FRIED GREEN TOMATOES

Makes 4 Slices

¼ cup yellow cornmeal
4 tablespoons panko bread
    crumbs
Vegetable oil for frying
1 large green tomato (or two
    small ones), cored and sliced
    into 4–5 thick slices
½ teaspoon coriander seed
1 teaspoon black pepper
¼ teaspoon garlic powder
¼ teaspoon onion powder
1 teaspoon kosher salt
¼ cup dry tempura mix
¼ cup prepared tempura batter
    (you will have some leftover)
¼ cup Founding Farmers green
    goddess dressing (p. 84)
¼ cup goat cheese, softened

Combine cornmeal and panko in a food processor and blend until fine. Set aside.

Add 1½ inches of vegetable frying oil to a large skillet and heat until very hot (preferably 350°F). Season the tomato slices on both sides with coriander, pepper, garlic powder, onion powder, and salt. Then bread tomatoes in the following order: dry tempura mix, prepared tempura batter, cornmeal/panko mix.

Place each breaded tomato slice very carefully into the hot oil (using a splatter screen will reduce the oil splatter). Fry until golden brown on one side. Flip and fry until the other side is golden brown. Remove from oil to a paper bag or to a paper towel-lined plate to drain. Portion the green goddess dressing and soft goat cheese into small bowls or ramekins. Shingle tomato slices on a plate and serve with the dips.

GREEN GODDESS DRESSING

Makes 2 Cups

½ cup finely chopped shallots

7 tablespoons extra-virgin olive oil

1 tablespoon minced garlic

4½ teaspoons white wine vinegar

2¼ teaspoons fresh lemon juice

2¼ teaspoons fresh lime juice

1 anchovy, diced fine

1 ripe avocado, skin and pit removed

½ cup mayonnaise

4 tablespoons fresh parsley, de-stemmed and chopped fine

3 tablespoons fresh tarragon, de-stemmed and chopped fine

1 tablespoon fresh cilantro, de-stemmed and chopped fine

2 tablespoons fresh basil, de-stemmed and chopped fine

¾ teaspoon fresh oregano, de-stemmed and chopped fine

1 teaspoon kosher salt

⅛ teaspoon black pepper

In a small skillet, sauté the shallots in 1 tablespoon of oil and set aside to cool. In a small mixing bowl, combine the garlic with the vinegar and lemon and lime juices and let macerate for 15 minutes. Add the anchovy and avocado.

Mash the avocado with a fork. Whisk in the mayonnaise and then slowly whisk in the remaining 6 tablespoons of olive oil. When the dressing is emulsified (thick like a dip), fold in the herbs, cooled shallots, and salt, and pepper to taste.

BEIGNETS

Makes Twenty 1-Ounce Beignets

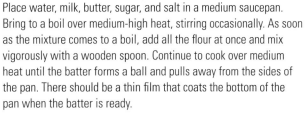

½ cup water
½ cup skim milk
½ cup unsalted butter
1 tablespoon granulated sugar
¼ teaspoon kosher salt
1¼ cups all-purpose flour
5 eggs
Vegetable oil for frying
Powdered sugar for sprinkling

Place water, milk, butter, sugar, and salt in a medium saucepan. Bring to a boil over medium-high heat, stirring occasionally. As soon as the mixture comes to a boil, add all the flour at once and mix vigorously with a wooden spoon. Continue to cook over medium heat until the batter forms a ball and pulls away from the sides of the pan. There should be a thin film that coats the bottom of the pan when the batter is ready.

Transfer the batter to a mixing bowl and mix on low speed for 30 seconds to release excess steam. Add eggs slowly, one at a time, allowing time between each addition for the eggs to incorporate. Scrape the sides of the bowl between additions. Once all of the eggs are incorporated, allow the batter to mix on low for 1 more minute. Place plastic wrap over batter, making sure it touches the surface of the batter, and let rest for at least 20 minutes.

Meanwhile, heat vegetable oil in a large, heavy pot or deep skillet (preferably to 325°F as this is the best temperature for the beignets). Using a 1 fluid ounce scoop (the size of about 2 tablespoons), drop balls of beignet batter into the hot oil. Allow to fry for 20 minutes, turning beignets over occasionally. Beignets are done when they are dark brown and crisp on the outside and cooked and airy on the inside. Drain on paper towels and toss with powdered sugar before serving. Serve warm with your favorite sweet dipping sauces (like chocolate, caramel, and raspberry).

Note: For both recipes, keep your batters cold and your oil clean.

OW, "GOOD STUFF" IS

DECLARATION, AN INS

SE GOOD STUFF EATERY

ON A MISSION TO BR

GOOD PEOPLE AND GOO

Good Stuff Eatery

The Good Stuff Eatery, like all of Spike Mendelsohn's ventures, is a family affair. Mendelsohn's mom inspired him to create a spot where people could pop in and order really good handcrafted burgers, fries, and milk shakes. Both his mom and his dad came out of retirement from their restaurant careers in Canada to launch the Capitol Hill eatery with him, and the former Top Chef contestant's sister, whom he describes as his "partner in crime," found the location for the Capitol Hill shop and handles many other parts of the business. A host of cousins, aunts, uncles, and close friends round out the rest of the support team.

"One thing that has never changed for me is that this business, the restaurant business, is the epitome of family," the Good Stuff Eatery owner often says.

Mendelsohn moved to DC in 2008, in the height of election season, and he couldn't resist the chance to hold an election burger challenge pitting a McCain burger against an Obama burger. The Obama burger won the Good Eatery contest 4-to-1, and if you don't know how the real election turned out you must reside under a very large, very remotely located rock. In a hamburger-imitating-life moment, the forty-fourth president of the United States stopped by the restaurant when he was in office to grab some grub for a pre-birthday celebration before he hit the big Five-O. While President Obama did not order the applewood bacon, onion marmalade, and horseradish mayo–topped burger that bears his name, he did, by all reports, enjoy every bite of his Good Stuff meal. Although President Obama no longer resides at 1600 Pennsylvania Avenue, his burger still graces the menu at 303 Pennsylvania Avenue.

303 Pennsylvania Avenue SE, Washington, DC 20003, (202) 543-8222, goodstuffeatery.com

PREZ OBAMA BURGER

Serves 6

FOR THE HORSERADISH MAYONNAISE:

2 cups basic mayonnaise
4 ounces prepared horseradish
1 tablespoon cayenne
1½ teaspoons freshly ground black pepper
Sea salt

FOR THE RED ONION MARMALADE:

2 red onions
1 cup Lucini Pinot Noir Italian wine vinegar
1 cup sugar

FOR THE BURGERS:

30 ounces ground sirloin
6 potato buns, cut in half
Canola oil
1 pound applewood-smoked bacon
Sea salt
Freshly ground black pepper
1 pound crumbled blue cheese

To prepare the horseradish mayonnaise: Add the basic mayonnaise, horseradish, cayenne, pepper, and salt to taste to a food processor or blender. Puree until smooth. The mayonnaise can be refrigerated in an airtight container for up to 1 week. This recipe yields about 2½ cups.

To prepare the red onion marmalade: Slice both red onions ½-inch thick. Add the vinegar and sugar to a pot over medium heat. Bring to a simmer. Once the sugar is completely dissolved, add the onions. Cook, stirring occasionally to prevent burning, until the onions are translucent and the liquid is reduced by half, about 5 minutes. Set aside to cool.

To prepare the burger patties: Roll six 5-ounce sirloin balls and form each ball into a patty. Arrange on a tray, cover, and refrigerate.

Toast the buns.

Heat a large skillet over medium-high heat and add just enough oil to cover the entire bottom of the pan. Line a plate with paper towels. When the oil begins to smoke, add the bacon and cook until crisp. Remove with a slotted spoon and drain on the paper towels. Drain the fat from the pan but do not wipe clean. Reduce the heat to medium and place the patties into the skillet. Season the patties with salt and pepper and cook for 3 minutes. Flip and cook on the other side for 1 minute more. Distribute the crumbled blue cheese equally among the patties and continue to cook 2 minutes more for medium-rare doneness. Cover with a lid for the last 30 seconds to melt the cheese.

To assemble the burgers: Place one patty on one bun bottom. Top the patty with some mayonnaise, marmalade, and bacon. Cover with the bun top. Repeat with the remaining patties.

H Street Conntry Clnb

When you're having a Washington-takes-itself-too-seriously day, get thee to the H Street Country Club. Do not pass go. Do not collect $200 in campaign donations. And, for the love of politics, do not have one more where-do-you-work-who-do-you-know-inside-the-Beltway conversation. Instead go directly to the H Street Corridor to trade in that [insert the name of your very impressive employer] badge around your neck for a Skee-ball, mini-golf putter, and cold beer.

With its tongue-in-cheek moniker, The H Street Country Club is a no-vetting-process-required hangout that serves Mexican food and drink against the backdrop of boardwalk-style games. Upstairs is a DC-themed mini golf course that looks like Willy Wonka and the Mad Hatter designed it on a dare. Actually, the course comes from the imagination and creative hands of local artist Lee Wheeler, who is responsible for the this-side-of-crazy-brilliant functional installation and all the other whimsy-with-an-edge art pieces throughout the multilevel bar. Favorite holes include King Kong scaling the Washington Monument, the zombie presidents (where Lincoln and several of his Oval Office successors join the ranks of the undead), and a poignant 3-D silhouette of the Iwo Jima Memorial fashioned out of more than a thousand plastic toy army men. Extra points for finding the tiny replicas of the Lincoln Theatre and Ben's Chili Bowl near the first putt and the face of infamous former DC mayor Marion Barry on the Awakening statue emerging from Astroturf near one of the last ones.

Unlike a PGA tournament, you can sip cocktails along the green. Tables are nearby, in addition to the ones downstairs and outside, where you can order off the menu that was crafted in conjunction with James Beard Award–winning chef Ann Cashion when the restaurant first opened.

1335 H Street, NE, Washington, DC 20002, (202) 399-4722, hstcountryclub.com

DORADO WITH JALAPEÑO LIME SAUCE

Serves 6

2 tablespoons finely diced red onions

3 jalapeños, seeded and finely diced*

2 sprigs of thyme

3 bay leaves

Juice of 15 limes

1½ cups white wine

1 pound asparagus

2 pounds fresh baby carrots

3 pounds of dorado (mahi-mahi), cut into 8-ounce pieces

Salt and pepper to taste

4 tablespoons blended oil (vegetable/olive oil)

8 ounces (2 sticks) butter, plus 1 tablespoon to sauté fish

4 tablespoons heavy whipping cream

To prepare the sauce: Combine the red onions, jalapeños, thyme, bay leaves, lime juice, and white wine in a small pot and reduce on low heat until you are left with about ⅕ of the initial volume. Set aside.

To prepare the vegetables: Peel and remove the bottom end of the asparagus (about 2 inches) on a diagonal cut. Cut the asparagus into pieces about 2½ inches long and blanch by placing in a pot of boiling water for 3 minutes. Immediately remove them and place them in ice water (this will help keep the green color and will stop the cooking process).

For the carrots: Peel and then repeat the blanching process. Set the vegetables to the side.

To prepare the fish: Sprinkle the fish with salt and pepper to taste. Heat a medium-sized pan over medium-high heat and add the oil. When the oil is hot, place the fish in the pan and sauté until the bottom is golden brown. Flip the fish once and cook until both sides are golden brown (about 4 minutes per side, depending on thickness), set aside, and cook the remaining pieces the same way.

When your fish is cooked, take the asparagus and carrots and lightly sauté them with a tablespoon of butter and a pinch of salt and pepper. Then bring your lime reduction back to a high flame and add the heavy whipping cream. When this mixture starts to boil, remove from the fire and add the butter little by little, mixing constantly with a whisk (do not stop whisking or your sauce will separate) until all of it is nicely incorporated into a silky sauce.

To assemble: Now that all the pieces for this puzzle are ready, put them together. Set the carrots and asparagus on the middle of the plate, place the piece of dorado right on top of them, and drizzle the lime and jalapeño sauce around that.

*For a spicier dish add more jalapeños.

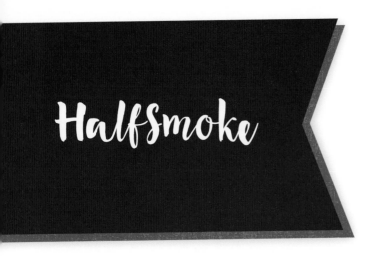

HalfSmoke

In 2013 Andre McCain left his high-powered finance job to work at McDonald's. "My friends thought I was crazy," says the owner of Shaw's HalfSmoke. "But I actually enjoyed it. That was the craziest part."

The unorthodox career turn was part of McCain's plan to start a business he had been cooking up in his imagination, a restaurant for grownups that evokes the nostalgia of childhood. It also was the next step in honoring the entrepreneurial talent McCain first sharpened as DC high school student.

Born and raised in Northeast DC's Deanwood neighborhood, Andre took a class while a student at Woodrow Wilson High School that he credits with changing his life. It was a seminar in entrepreneurship that taught him how to create a business plan, raise funds, and the other steps necessary to launch a new commercial endeavor. Through the class, he competed and placed in a national start-up business competition for high schoolers and found a community of investors and colleagues, some of whom years later helped him launch Half Smoke.

A young McCain first flexed his entrepreneurial muscles while still at Wilson in the form of Break Your Neck Kicks. Break Your Neck Kicks came about from his observations about the early days of internet shopping. McCain would search for bargain deals on the popular styles and brands of sneakers and then resell them to his classmates for a profit. He made about $100,000 from the venture.

"It was back in the 56k dial-in days of the Internet," he explains. "It was the wild, wild west. The price in DC [of shoes] was very, very different than the price in Russia or Oakland. The Internet made it possible to find good deals if you know where to look."

McCain clearly knew where to look. He also knew where to look when he was ready to start HalfSmoke. He spent a summer working at three fast food chains – McDonald's, Sweetgreen, and Pret A Manger. It served as his crash course in all things restaurants. He did everything from cleaning bathrooms, to filling orders, to helping with the books. Armed with that experience, the native Washingtonian began what turned into a three-year process of securing funding for his concept. A concept that he points out that also has DC roots.

"When I was growing up, our weekend ritual was to go to the farmers market [at RFK stadium] and get a half smoke," he says. "I always associated it with something happy. Our menu tries to capture childhood. Our restaurant takes the nostalgia of childhood and replicates it in a way that adults can enjoy."

No surprise, the star of the HalfSmoke menu is half smokes. Other memory-laden favorites include funnel cakes, sweet potato tots, and the good-as-they-look crazy milkshakes. Local beers and cocktails are served from the full bar that hopefully does not carry childhood memories for most customers.

The feel of the large restaurant carries the fun of an old quick serve or fast food spots of days gone by while still offering table service. Games, funky couches, and a photo booth fill the space. Families, millennials, and college students, many from nearby Howard University, all gravitate to HalfSmoke and the signatures crazy milkshakes. As it is with most good things in life, the secret seems to be in that thick layer of sweet gooey icing.

"We often get milkshakes left over but never frosting," says General Manager Alfio Celia. "It's always licked clean."

651 Florida Ave NW, Washington, DC 20001, halfsmoke.com

MILKY CEREAL SUPER MILKSHAKE
AKA THEN THERE WAS PEBBLES (TIMES WAS ROUGH)

Serves 1

1 cup Vanilla ice cream
¾ cup Whole milk
2 tablespoons Strawberry sauce
2 tablespoons or more vanilla
　　icing for rim of glass, chilled
2 tablespoons Fruity Pebble
　　dust plus 1 tablespoon of the
　　cereal to add to the ice cream
Whipped cream for topping
1 piece Rice Krispy Treat
1 piece
Tablespoon Fruit Loops

Scoop cold (warm icing does not stick well) vanilla icing with a spoon and apply a thick layer of icing on the rim of a milkshake-specific glass (eg, wide mouth and narrow base).

Crush Fruity Pebbles in a sealed Ziploc bag, and then pour Pebble "dust" onto a flat plate. Roll glass in crushed Pebble "dust" so icing rim is fully covered.

Blend vanilla ice cream and whole milk together along with 1 tablespoon of Fruity Pebbles to desired thickness in a durable cup (ideally in a milkshake-specific blender, but a regular blender is also fine).

Pour milkshake into glass, about 80 percent of the way. Apply a generous amount of whipped cream to the top of the glass. Squeeze strawberry sauce onto whipped cream tower using broad strokes. Apply Fruit Loops cereal to top of whipped cream tower. Add half a Rice Krispy Treat to the side of the glass, standing up for vertical height. Add 1–2 straws.

Serve and be happy.

härth

Chef Tom Elder liked to take to the open road during his stint at härth (he has since left härth). Atop his self-described Steve McQueen–style motorcycle, he rode through the Shenandoah Valley visiting the farmers and the land that continue to help stock the restaurant's kitchen with fresh goods while at the same time soaking up hearty helpings of inspiration. For Elder, this kind of two-wheeled ritual wasn't about gimmicks or photo ops. It's just how he rolls, so to speak. It's also how he has built a menu with a true local soul at härth, his Tysons Corner restaurant.

"When we were getting started we said, let's put ourselves as part of the community," says the former executive chef of härth, housed in the funky Hilton McLean, "Virginia is such fertile ground. When we were getting started we thought we could actually build a real regional cuisine here."

Elder worked with many cooperatives and regional producers to do this and even started the tradition of raising honeybees on one of the low roofs at the hotel. He got the idea to start beekeeping after a discussion he had with some colleagues about how there were no zucchini blossoms that year because there weren't enough honeybees around. "We wanted to do something to be part of the community," he tells.

Now the hives, produce some 200 pounds of honey a year, Restaurant staff that tend to the bees regularly move the hives to make sure they get the right amount of sunlight, keep tabs on the queen, and extract honeycomb. The honey produced can be sampled in the signature bacon jam, and on the cheese and charcuterie trays. You can even stir some into your tea. Furthering the restaurants commitment to the community, the bees sometimes go on the road from time to time in a heavy-duty acrylic carrying case he designed for the purpose. The chefs sometimes take the bees around to schools to help educate children on healthy eating. And, so they can see that honey doesn't come from plastic squeeze bears.

7920 Jones Branch Drive, McLean, Virginia 22102, (703) 847-5000, hiltonmclean.com/harth

CRAB FONDUE

Serves 2–4

1 tablespoon onions, minced
1 clove roasted garlic, minced
   (see instructions below)
1 tablespoon butter
2 ounces fresh baby spinach,
   roughly chopped
½ cup heavy whipping cream
3 tablespoons grated Asiago
   cheese
1 tablespoon grated Parmesan
   cheese
1 tablespoon sour cream
1 teaspoon kosher salt
½ teaspoon black pepper
4 ounces Maryland lump
   crabmeat, freshly steamed

ROASTED GARLIC
½ cup vegetable oil
1 head of fresh garlic, whole
   cloves, skin peeled
½ teaspoon kosher salt
¼ teaspoon freshly ground black
   pepper

To prepare the fondue: Sauté the onions and roasted garlic in the butter. Add the spinach and lightly wilt.

Then add the cream and bring to a boil. Simmer for 10 minutes. Add both cheeses and stir until they are incorporated. Stir in the sour cream and season well with salt and pepper. Fold in the steamed crabmeat. Serve in a casserole dish on top of a base plate. Serve with rustic bread cut into chunks or cubes and arranged on the base plate.

To prepare the roasted garlic: Heat the oil in small ovenproof saucepan over a medium heat. Place the garlic in the oil and season with salt and pepper. Place foil over top of pan and place into 300°F oven. Bake for 20 minutes. Check garlic, it should be golden brown. Remove the roasted garlic from oil with slotted spoon and place into a small ceramic plate. Let cool.

Use 1 clove or more (to taste) for the crab fondue recipe above.

Strain the oil into a small metal or ceramic container and allow it to cool. Once cooled you can store the oil in the refrigerator. The oil can be used for other recipes as can the extra garlic.

What's the Buzz

A Q &A with Photographer Emily Pearl Goodstein about Capturing the Black and Yellow Beast on Film

Have you ever photographed bees or other stinging insects before?

This was my first foray into the field of insect photography. With the exception of the special gear, it is actually a very similar experience to photographing babies and toddlers— lots of running around and quick camera decisions.

Were you nervous?

Yes! About twenty-four hours before the shoot, I started to get nervous. My main concern was about a bee getting inside the bee suit. I brought a friend along so she could drive me to the emergency room in case anything bad happened. But once I got on the roof in my suit with my camera in hand, things were actually pretty peaceful (yet very hot).

What was it like to wear a bee suit?

The bee suit is perhaps the most unflattering item I have ever worn. It is also very hot inside there. There are lots of pockets and lots of elastic at the ankles and wrists. The whole getup looked even better when paired with the dish gloves I wore to protect my hands while I was manipulating my camera.

Can you really tell the difference between the bees?

At first glance, I couldn't tell the difference but once Chef Tom pointed out who was who, I could really tell that the queen bee was a little larger than the others. She was also surrounded by the worker bees. The other interesting thing is that the honeycombs filled with honey are sort of white, not clear or yellowish as you'd expect. This was confusing at first because I wasn't sure if the bees had been very productive, but then Chef Tom explained where the honey was and where the honeycombs were empty.

Were any of the bees camera shy? Did the Queen hog the lens?

All the bees actually stayed away from the camera. I was expecting them to buzz around me and my gear, but as Chef Tom described it, his bees are very mellow.

Hula Girl Bar and Grill

Mikala Brennan knows better than to question the power of the Spam. The self-described Hula Girl food-truck chef turned brick-and-mortar Hula Girl Bar and Grill owner can't really explain the fascination with the canned meat but always sold a huge amount of it each week from her aloha-ed out surfboard-topped mobile Hawaiian restaurant.

Even with the two-per-customer limit during her Hula Girl Food Truck days, Hula Girl's spam musubi sold out just about each day that Brennan takes to the streets of DC with her truck filled with authentic Hawaiian food. It continues to be a perennial favorite at the Arlington restaurant. Found almost everywhere in the islands from convenience stores to school cafeterias to the zoo, the rectangular snack basically is a fried piece of Spam over rice that is pressed together and wrapped with seaweed. "It's salty, it's savory, and it's oddly addictive," says the Oahu native Brennan. "It's one of those things you can go and grab at pretty much any 7-Eleven at home. It's portable. It's something that doesn't need to be refrigerated. It's even something of a rite of passage for newcomers who want to attain local status to eat a Spam musubi."

Hula Girl's offerings hardly are limited to the Hawaiian preserved-meat delicacy. She also serves teriyaki steak, chicken, and tofu that can be ordered over a salad in a banh mi–style sandwich or as a plate lunch island-style with two scoops of rice and a scoop of her fabulous macaroni salad. Brennan spent months and months perfecting her teriyaki to get it just right and up to her Hawaiian standards. The Kalua Pork also transports Hawaiians thousands of miles back home with its authentic flavors. Kalua, Brennan tells, is derived from two words in Hawaiian—ka meaning "the" and lua meaning "hole," which refers to the use of an underground oven or imu. Although she promises she does not dig holes on the Mall to cook

her pork, she has mastered the art of re-creating the taste from five thousand miles away. She has done such a good job that Brennan has counted the Hawaiian congressional delegation and staff members among her followers, along with many, many others with aloha in their hearts and on their minds.

The cocktails served at the restaurant are island-approved, as is everything on the menu made by her kitchen staff that is almost all women, a rarity in the restaurant world.

4044 Campbell Ave, Arlington, VA 22206, hulagirlbarandgrill.com

You won't find hot sauce lined up with the condiments at Hula Girl but a steady supply of Hawaiian Chili Water, ginger, garlic, salt and chili peppers blended with water and a splash of vinegar, will always be on hand to spice up any dish. "We don't really have hot sauce in Hawaii because we don't have a lot of vinegars there," Brennan explains. "But we use lots and lots of chili water. We have it out on the table where the Tabasco would go."

SPAM MUSUBI
Makes 10 Musubi

4 cups Calrose rice (sushi rice is
    a good substitute)
4 cups water
Sushi vinegar (recipe below)
1 tablespoon furikake (a
    seasoning mix of nori,
    sesame seeds, salt, and
    sugar easily found in Asian
    markets)
5 sheets of roasted nori or
    Korean laver
¼ cup soy sauce
1 teaspoon sugar
1 can Spam

FOR THE SUSHI VINEGAR:
1 cup rice wine vinegar
½ cup sugar
1 tablespoon kosher salt

Place rice in a saucepan with water. Wash rice by stirring with your hand and replacing the water until it remains clear. Drain rice in colander, transfer to a heavy pot or rice cooker, and add 4 cups of water. Heat over medium-high heat and bring just to a boil. Reduce heat to low and simmer, covered, for 15 minutes. Turn off heat and leave pan covered for 15 additional minutes. Place the rice in a bowl and let it cool completely. Add 2 tablespoons of the sushi vinegar and the furikake to the rice and mix thoroughly with your hands.

Cut nori in half widthwise—this will give you 10 sheets. Mix soy sauce and sugar and hold.

Cut Spam into 10 rectangular slices about ¼-inch thick. In a large, ungreased frying pan over medium heat, fry slices until brown and slightly crispy. With the pan still hot, add the soy sauce and sugar mixture and slightly braise the Spam in the liquid. Put aside.

Using a musubi press, place a nori piece onto a cutting board. Position press on top of the nori so the length of the press is in the middle of the nori (widthwise). The press and the width of the nori should fit exactly the length of a slice of Spam. (Note: If you don't have a musubi press, you can use the empty Spam can by opening both sides, creating a musubi mold.)

Spread approximately ¼ cup cooked rice across the bottom of the musubi maker, on top of the nori. Press rice down with flat part of the press to compact the rice. Place a slice of Spam on top of the rice (it should cover most of the length of the musubi maker). Cover with an additional ¼ cup of rice. Remove the musubi from the press by pushing the whole stack down (with the flat part of the press) while lifting off the press. Fold one end of nori over the musubi and press lightly onto the rice.

Repeat with the other Spam slices.

Do not refrigerate musubi, as they will get dry and rubbery.

To prepare the sushi vinegar: Heat the rice wine vinegar in a small saucepan. Add the sugar and salt. Stir until dissolved. Let cool down and hold for use. You can refrigerate the sushi vinegar for up to 2 weeks in an airtight container.

KALUA PORK

1 cup canola oil
½ cup Hawaiian salt (kosher salt can be used)
2 tablespoons all-natural liquid smoke (can be found in natural food stores)
2 fresh banana leaves (can be found in Asian markets)
10 pounds pork butt

Preheat the oven to 500°F.

Take ¼ cup of the oil and mix with the salt and liquid smoke to make a paste. Set aside.

Lay a piece of heavy-duty aluminum foil (approximately 18 x 18 inches) onto a work surface. Place one of the banana leaves onto the foil. Take your paste and spread half of this onto the banana leaves. Place pork onto the top of this, then use the remaining paste and rub the pork really well on the top. Use the other banana leaf on the top of the pork. Place another piece of foil on the top of the banana leaf. Then pull the bottom and top sheets of foil together to create a tight seal.

Place foil package into a large roasting pan, fill with 2 inches of water, then cover the pan with foil to seal in the steam.

Place the pork into the oven and drop the temperature down to 350°F. Roast pork in oven until very tender when pierced with fork, about 5 hours.

Remove the pan from the oven and let cool slightly. Unwrap the foil carefully as there will be steam wanting to escape. Discard the banana leaves. Pull the pork out of the roasting pan—but reserve the juices! Shred the pork with two forks or with tongs. Add in some of the reserved juices.

Serve with some sticky rice and veggies for a great meal.

The pork can be refrigerated for up to 5 days.

The Inn at Little Washington

Gregorian chants float through the air at The Inn at Little Washington's Windsor Castle–inspired kitchen as chefs clad in Dalmatian-print pants move through the space with the grace and study typically reserved for prima ballerinas. Every item down to the smallest of measuring spoons has a purpose and place here, where calm is the objective and a dash of whimsy folded into large quantities of perfection is the secret ingredient. This level of precision and creativity is what has made a table at The Inn at Little Washington one of the area's—and the country's—most sought-after reservations and the recipient of two coveted Michelin stars.

"Happy people make happy food" stands as the mantra here at Chef Patrick O'Connell's kitchen, often described as being one of the most beautiful in the world. Hand-painted blue-and-white Portuguese tiles grace the walls along with a portrait of the chef and his beloved dogs, the same ones whose memory are honored with the black-and-white spots on the chef's uniforms. The strings of pearls worn by the female servers also serve as an homage to the chef's dogs, one of whom was named Pearl. As you might imagine, when both pampered pooches were alive, they ate well and even feasted on the first truffles of the season. One more example of how living and eating well is woven into the fabric of the restaurant.

"I've worked in a lot of 'hell's kitchens' and found them to be counterproductive environments that tend to short circuit the creative process," tells O'Connell. "We refer to The Inn at Little Washington as 'heaven's kitchen' and try to maintain a calm and relaxed work space. This helps reduce accidents, contributes to staff retention, and, we think, it makes the food taste better."

While the surroundings and spirit of the inn cannot be denied, the food is why legions of people make a pilgrimage to The Inn at Little Washington a must on their foodie bucket list. The menu is ever-changing, based on the bounty of the day and the imagination of those working in the kitchen. O'Connell's recipe for Lamb Carpaccio with Caesar Salad Ice Cream, which he shares here, is a decadent example of why so many mark the most special of special occasions at the restaurant.

309 Middle Street, Washington, VA 22747, (540) 675-3800, theinnatlittlewashington.com

CARPACCIO OF HERB-CRUSTED BABY LAMB
WITH CAESAR SALAD ICE CREAM

Serves 6

FOR THE PESTO:

2 cups packed fresh basil leaves

¼ cup pine nuts

¼ cup fresh parsley leaves

2 garlic cloves, roughly chopped

⅓ cup extra-virgin olive oil

½ cup freshly grated Parmesan
  cheese, preferably grated on
  a microplane

½ teaspoon freshly squeezed
  lemon juice

Sugar, salt, and freshly ground
  pepper to taste

FOR THE CROUTONS:

2 cups vegetable or grape-seed
  oil

1 whole garlic clove, peeled

1 sprig fresh rosemary

6–8 slices of baguette or French
  bread, cut into 1-inch cubes
  (approximately 2 cups)

Salt to taste

To prepare the pesto: In a blender or food processor combine the basil, pine nuts, parsley, and garlic. Puree until smooth. With the motor running add the olive oil in a thin stream.

Add the Parmesan and then season to taste with the lemon juice, sugar, salt, and pepper. Keep refrigerated until ready to use.

To prepare the croutons: In a heavy, 1-quart saucepan over medium-high heat, heat the oil to about 350°F. Add the garlic clove to season the oil. Once the clove is golden brown but not burned, remove from the oil and discard. Add the sprig of rosemary and fry for 30 seconds or so, then remove and discard.

Add the croutons in two batches and fry until golden brown. Remove the croutons from the oil with a slotted spoon or spider and drain on paper towels. Season with salt. Set aside until ready to use.

FOR THE LAMB CARPACCIO:
1–1½ pounds of lamb loin, off the bone and trimmed of all sinew and fat
½ cup dried oregano
½ cup dried thyme
½ cup dried basil
½ cup dried tarragon
Grape-seed or vegetable oil for searing

FOR THE CAESAR DRESSING:
1 large egg yolk
6 tablespoons red wine vinegar
1 tablespoon fresh lemon juice
2 teaspoons Dijon mustard
1½ teaspoons Worcestershire sauce
¼ cup grated Parmesan cheese
1 large garlic clove, minced
1 anchovy fillet, minced
Pinch of cayenne
⅓ cup extra-virgin olive oil
¼ cup salad or vegetable oil
Salt and freshly ground pepper to taste

To prepare the lamb carpaccio: Season the lamb loin with salt and pepper and allow it to rest at room temperature for 15 minutes.

In a small bowl combine the herbs. Coat the loin with the mixture.

In a heavy-bottom or cast-iron skillet over medium-high heat, add the grape-seed oil until it is about ⅛–¼ inch deep. Once hot, add the loin and evenly sear the lamb on all sides.

Remove from the pan and allow to cool, preferably on a rack. Once cooled, wrap in plastic wrap and freeze until ready to use. (Freezing allows you to get paper-thin slices.)

To prepare the dressing: Combine the yolk, vinegar, lemon juice, mustard, Worcestershire, Parmesan, garlic, anchovies, and cayenne in a food processor or blender. With the motor running, add the oils in a thin stream. Season with salt and pepper. Reserve in the refrigerator until ready to use. The dressing will keep up to 4 days.

To prepare the Caesar salad ice cream: In a large bowl, whisk together the yolks and sugar. In a large saucepan over medium heat combine the milk, powdered milk, Parmesan cheese, anchovies, and garlic and bring just to a boil, stirring constantly.

Place the egg yolk mixture in the top of a double boiler and slowly whisk in the hot milk mixture. Set the mixture over a pot of simmering water and whisk until the mixture thickens enough to coat the back of a spoon.

Remove the mixture from heat and let cool. Whisk in Worcestershire, Dijon, and season with salt and pepper to taste.

Freeze in an ice cream maker according to the manufacturer's instructions. The ice cream can keep in the freezer for up to a month or until ready to serve.

To assemble: Spread 1 tablespoon of pesto in an arc across the corner of the plate.

Scoop the Caesar ice cream into small balls and keep in the freezer until ready to serve.

Remove the lamb from the freezer and cut into paper-thin slices. Arrange the slices into four or five overlapping rows in the center of six chilled serving plates.

Sprinkle the lamb with the red onion slices, capers, chives, croutons, and arugula.

In a medium bowl, toss the lettuce leaves with enough of the Caesar dressing to thoroughly coat and place the leaves on the corner opposite the pesto. Sprinkle generously with Parmesan cheese.

Scatter 3–4 small scoops of Caesar ice cream across the lamb and serve immediately.

FOR THE CAESAR SALAD ICE CREAM:

7 large egg yolks
⅓ cup sugar
4⅓ cups whole milk
¾ cup powdered milk
1⅓ cups freshly grated Parmesan cheese
4 anchovy fillets, minced
2 tablespoons minced garlic
1 tablespoon Worcestershire sauce
2 tablespoons Dijon mustard
Salt and pepper to taste

3 red pearl onions, peeled and sliced in paper-thin rings
1 tablespoon capers
2 tablespoons finely chopped chives
½ cup baby arugula leaves, washed
6 leaves from a heart of romaine lettuce
½ cup grated Parmesan cheese

Jaleo DC

Choosing a table at the downtown Jaleo almost is as fun as choosing what to eat.

If you feel like playing with your food, head to one of the custom-designed working foosball tables near the front of the restaurant, complete with artist-made figurines—one set is men vs. women and the other is traditional Spanish dolls, like a flamenco dancer and bullfighters. The stools surrounding the tables are created from Vespa scooter seats. If you have romance on the mind, reserve one of the love tables tucked away behind floor-to-ceiling metal curtains for extra privacy. And, for days when you are feeling chatty and outgoing, head to one of the communal tables surrounded by an assortment of different chairs, including one crafted from recycled plastic.

"Everything here in the space has a story, from the hanging lights created from books, to the oversized original murals of people on the go, to a masked bull head that watches over guests.

The food here also tells a story of José Andrés's vision of a tapas restaurant that reflects the rich regional diversity of classical and contemporary Spanish cuisine. Chef Ramon Martinez who helped create these dishes stresses the importance of using good quality extra-virgin olive oil when you make these recipes at home and premium Spanish anchovies. He adds that many Americans that think they don't like anchovies change their minds after they finally try the Spanish ones. "It's like they are tasting them for the first time," Martinez says.

480 7th Street NW, Washington, DC 20004, (202) 628-7949, jaleo.com

ESCALIBADA CATALANA CON ANCHOAS
CATALAN ROASTED VEGETABLES WITH ANCHOVIES
Serves 6

ROASTED VEGETABLES:
1 large eggplant
2 red bell peppers
2 tablespoons Spanish extra-
   virgin olive oil
Kosher salt to taste
1 large Vidalia onion, peeled and
   cut into 1-inch slices

ESCALIBADA DRESSING:
1 cup roasted vegetable juice
   (reserved from roasted
   vegetables)
1½ cups Spanish extra-virgin
   olive oil
½ cup Spanish sherry vinegar
Kosher salt to taste

9 premium quality Spanish
   anchovy fillets
Sea salt to taste
2 tablespoons chopped parsley

To prepare the vegetables: Coat the eggplant and red pepper with the olive oil and sprinkle with salt. Cook on a grill over medium heat, making sure to turn the vegetables and cook evenly. Keep on the grill for about 30 minutes or until fully cooked.

Place the eggplant in one container and the red peppers in a separate container. Cover both containers with plastic and set aside for 20 minutes to steam.

Peel the eggplant and discard the skin. Cut the eggplant flesh into 1-inch wide strips and discard the seeds. Save the juice for later use.

Peel the red peppers and cut in 1-inch thick strips and set aside. Reserve the juice as well. Coat the onion with olive oil and salt. Roast in the oven for 20 minutes at 350°F. Once they are cooked and brown let cool and set aside until needed.

To prepare the dressing: In a small pot, reduce the roasted vegetable juice by half and set aside. In a bowl, combine the vegetable juice reduction, olive oil, and vinegar then whisk. Adjust salt to taste and save for later use.

To serve: On a plate, place the roasted eggplant and pepper slices. Top with the roasted onions and the anchovy fillets. Generously dress with the escalibada dressing. Season with salt, garnish with the herbs, and serve.

GAMBAS AL AJILLO
SAUTÉED SHRIMP WITH GARLIC AND GUINDILLA PEPPER

Serves 5

SAUTÉED SHRIMP:

4 cloves of garlic, peeled

¼ cup Spanish extra-virgin Olive Oil

5 Arbol chilis

1 pound jumbo shrimp, peeled and deveined (or your preferred size)

5 tablespoons of brandy

5 tablespoons lemon Juice

½ cup brava sauce (recipe below)

Kosher salt to taste

BRAVA SAUCE:

2 tablespoons vegetable oil

1 ounce whole garlic, peeled and sliced

2 Arbol chilis

2 tablespoons sugar

2 tablespoons Spanish sherry vinegar

1 tablespoon tomato paste

2 pounds whole canned tomatoes (pureed)

1 tablespoon Spanish sweet pimenton

Kosher salt to taste

2 tablespoons chopped parsley

To prepare the shrimp: Thinly slice the garlic cloves with a knife, mandoline, or slicer and set aside. In a large skillet, heat the oil over medium heat. Add the garlic and cook until it begins to fry. Add the Arbol chilis and cook for 1 minute. Turn the heat up to high and add the shrimp. When the shrimp starts to change color, add the brandy, lemon juice, and brava sauce then stir to combine. Remove from the heat, season with salt and serve.

To prepare the sauce: In a medium size pot over medium heat, add the oil, garlic, and Arbol chilis, and sauté slowly until they start to brown. Add the sugar and stir until it melts. Add the vinegar and tomato paste and cook for a few minutes. Pour in the tomato puree and simmer until almost dry. Add the pimenton and adjust seasoning with salt if necessary. Strain through a sieve and reserve for later use.

To serve: Stack the shrimp into 5 shallow bowls, garnish with the parsley and serve.

Kaz Sushi Bistro

Chef Kazuhiro "Kaz" Okochi's childhood memories of Nagoya, Japan, are dotted with recollections of cooking. In third grade he decided to surprise his mom by making her dinner on her birthday. The young boy made fried rice and flan from recipes he found on the back of the monthly school lunch menu. (She, of course, cried lots of happy mom tears.) In the fifth grade the future owner of a bistro bearing his name remembers attempting to bake cakes in his family's kitchen from recipes in his mother's cookbooks. (He didn't have the right electric mixer so they turned out kind of flat.) And, a few years later, even as sports and schoolwork took up most of his time, he remembers being obsessed with a television show called Cooking Heaven, where the head of a culinary school prepared different dishes for viewers at home.

"He was my idol," Okochi tells. "I later would go to his culinary school."

The inspiration for the Sea Trout Napoleon, something of a signature dish of his, is also a product of his memory. After he graduated from the esteemed Tsuji Culinary Institute in Osaka, Okochi got a job at a sushi restaurant. His owner took the team out a few times a year on holidays. On one particular occasion the group went out to a restaurant in Kobe's Chinatown, where they dined on a whole Thai snapper with sliced peanuts and cilantro. All these years later the dish still leaves an impression. "I still remembered the dish," he says. "I created this one based on my memory of it."

Fresh, high-quality fish stands as the key to creating Okochi 's homage to that Kobe meal long ago. If you can't find good trout he recommends substituting sea bass or a white-meat fish like flounder. The marinade can be prepared ahead but tossing the fish in the sauce and the final assembly needs to be done just before serving.

1915 Eye Street NW, Washington, DC 20006, (202) 234-5000, kazsushibistro.com

SEA TROUT NAPOLEON

Serves 4

FOR THE MARINADE:
1 tablespoon rice vinegar
3 tablespoons soy sauce
1 teaspoon sugar
1 tablespoon sesame oil
1 teaspoon chili sesame oil
¼ teaspoon chile powder
¼ teaspoon ginger juice

FOR THE FRIED WONTONS:
Vegetable oil, as needed for frying
8 wonton skins, cut into 2½-inch
    rounds

FOR THE BEET DRESSING:
2 tablespoons white balsamic
    vinegar
2 tablespoons rice vinegar
¼ cup canola oil
½ teaspoon sugar
1 tablespoon beet juice

FOR THE SEA TROUT:
1 (8-ounce) sea trout fillet,
    skinned and finely diced
2 tablespoons coarsely chopped
    unsalted peanuts
2 sprigs cilantro, stemmed and
    minced

FOR THE GARNISH:
Assorted red and green seaweed

To prepare the marinade: In a small bowl, combine all the ingredients and reserve.

To prepare the fried wontons: In a medium saucepan, heat about a ½-inch of oil to 400°F. Add the wonton skins, fry until golden brown and crisp, and remove to a paper towel–lined half sheet pan to drain and cool.

To prepare the beet dressing: In a small bowl, combine all the ingredients, whisking to incorporate, and set aside.

To prepare the sea trout: In a medium bowl, combine all of the ingredients including the marinade, tossing to incorporate right before serving.

To assemble the napoleon: Place half of the fried wontons on a flat work surface and spoon half of the sea trout on top. Place the remaining fried wontons on top, finishing with the remaining trout. Place a sea trout napoleon in the center of a plate, garnish with seaweed, and drizzle beet dressing.

Serve immediately.

The Liberty Tree

Scott Hamilton came down to DC after college for what he thought would be a short stint tending bar, and he never stopped. The New England native wound up opening Hamilton's Bar & Grill and moving into an apartment on H Street before the gastro real estate boom took hold. When it came time for his next venture, setting up a bar with great food close to home seemed like the right move.

The only question remaining was what to serve. A quick trip to his hometown near Cape Cod provided the answer. "I went home and spent about ten days up there eating a lot of seafood," he says. "Then we came up with a menu of simple comfort food with a flair based on the flavors up there."

The wildly popular White Cheddar Lobster Mac & Cheese showcases the original intent of the neighborhood spot. It's simple, crowd-pleasing, and is a nod to Hamilton's roots. The seafood-infused mac and cheese started out as just a side dish only meant to appear on the menu for a weekend, but customers kept sending word back to the kitchen that it needed to be a permanent Liberty Tree fixture. When attempting to make it at home, really good quality cheese and fresh lobster meat make all the difference.

Much like everything else served at the H Street hangout, the signature dish is made in house. "We make everything from scratch," Hamilton tells. "The only thing we buy is ketchup."

Sadly, The Liberty Tree recently closed, but we look forward to seeing where Hamilton's career takes him.

WHITE CHEDDAR LOBSTER MAC & CHEESE

Serves 6–8

FOR MAC AND CHEESE:

1 pound dried shell pasta

1 stick butter

½ cup all-purpose flour

3 cups heavy cream

2 cups shredded white cheddar
(Vermont, aged 2 years, if
possible)

2 tablespoons mascarpone
cheese

2 tablespoons grated pecorino
Romano

Salt and pepper

1½ pound lobster, boiled and
broken down into chunks

2 tablespoons truffle oil

½ bunch fresh chopped parsley
(garnish)

FOR PANKO TOPPING:

2 cups panko bread crumbs

¼ cup melted butter

¼ cup grated pecorino Romano

Preheat oven to 400°F. Boil salted water and cook pasta until al dente. Drain well and cool under cold running water. Set aside.

Melt butter slowly over medium heat, add flour to make a roux, stirring constantly until flour is incorporated. Cook for 5 minutes on low heat, stirring occasionally to keep it from burning. Add heavy cream, cheddar, mascarpone, and pecorino stirring over medium heat until everything is melted and smooth. Season with salt and pepper. Fold in lobster meat and cooked pasta. Transfer mixture to 8-ounce ramekins. Combine ingredients for panko topping and top the pasta with the mixture. Bake until well browned. Drizzle with truffle oil and fresh chopped parsley.

Little Coco's

Despite its Jersey Shore sounding name, fried pizza's pedigree traces back to Naples, not a boardwalk. Little Coco's Executive Chef Adam Harvey first discovered the deep-fried deliciousness on a research trip to Italy before opening the modern Italian eatery named for his wife.

"I took one bite and I knew," Harvey says of the moment he decided to include the delicacy on the Petworth restaurant's menu.

In Naples "pizza frito classico" is street food, a whole rolled up pizza served in a paper cone and sold from one of the many stands that dot the city's narrow streets. A less portable version makes an appearance at many of the sit-down pizzerias found in Southern Italy, which boasts the distinction of being the birthplace of pizza. At Little Coco's, Harvey's version is served in what looks like an evenly shaped croissant. He stuffs the dough with mozzarella and homemade tomato sauce, an homage to his in-laws family recipe, before dunking it in the fryer. Every one of the approximately hundred fried pizzas the restaurant makes each week is rolled by hand and made to order. Harvey assures the novice that with some practice, and a deep fryer or oversized pot, anyone can replicate the recipe at home.

"It's pretty simple," he says "It's dough, sauce, and cheese. You can make your own sauce or you can buy sauce. You can buy pizza dough or you can make your own. The only trick is to be gentle so you don't break the dough. A liquid starts to form when the cheese heats up. So if you pierce the dough the liquid spills out and you wind up with dirty oil and not a lot of filling left on the inside. It's really just patience and time."

3907 14th St NW, Washington, DC 20011, (202) 853-9889, littlecocos.com

PIZZA FRITO CLASSICO

PIZZA DOUGH

2 pounds 00 Caputo flour ("00"
    is a classification used in
    Italy to tell how fine a flour
    is ground. The 00 flour is
    highly refined and has the
    consistancy of soft powder.)
8 ounces semolina flour
2 ounces fresh yeast
20 grams sugar
34 grams salt
14 ounces beer
14 ounces cold water
20 grams honey
20 grams olive oil
Cooking spray

MARINARA SAUCE

2 10-ounce cans San Marzano
    (hand-crushed)
¼ cup red wine
1 tablespoon sugar
2 teaspoons salt
1 teaspoon red chili flakes
1 teaspoon black pepper
5 fresh basil sprigs

ADDITIONAL INGREDIENTS:

4 4-ounce fresh mozzarella balls
10 basil leaves, julienned
1 cup 00 flour (for dusting)

For pizza dough: Combine water, beer, yeast, honey and sugar and whisk for 1 minute. Combine semolina flour and salt. Add liquid to mixer, and then add dry ingredients. Add olive oil. Mix at low until combined for 1 minute; then at medium for 12 minutes. Place dough in container sprayed with cooking spray for 24 hours. Remove dough and portion into 10oz balls and place in refrigerator for 24 hours.

For the sauce: In a medium pot add all ingredients together. Bring sauce to a light simmer and cook for 30 minutes. Remove the basil sprigs from the sauce and let cool and refrigerate for at least 12 hours. Let sauce come to room temperature before use.

Assembly: Lightly flour a cutting board or your counter. Take one ball of dough at a time and stretch the dough by hand until it reaches 15" in diameter. You can always use a rolling pin if you can't stretch the dough with your hands.

Add 2oz. of room temperature marinara sauce to the bottom third of the dough.

Cut the mozzarella ball into 5 even slices and spread the cheese on top of the sauce in a fan pattern overlapping ½ inch over each piece of cheese.

Place 1 tablespoon of basil over the cheese.

Gently take the bottom of the dough and fold over the filling. Using the side of your hand push the dough tight to the filling. Then begin to roll the dough as tight as possible without piercing the dough.

Once you have rolled the pizza until there is 1 inch of space left us your finger and a little bit of water to wet the edge of the dough. Complete the rolling process. The water will give you a tight seal.

Grab the two ends of the dough and bring them together, to form a doughnut shape. Pinch the two ends together to seal. If you ends are too dry use a little water to help seal them together. Place the finished pizza on a lightly floured small plate to help move the pizza to the fryer.

In a deep fat fryer set to 350°F gently slide the pizza in the oil from the plate. The pizza will float to the top of the oil let it fry for 3 minutes; then flip the pizza and fry for an additional 3 minutes.

Remove the pizza from the oil and pat dry on a paper towel.

Place the fried pizza on a plate and drizzle with olive oil and sea salt. Serve fried pizza with a small salad of arugula dressed with olive oil and lemon juice and a side of warm marinara sauce.

Little Red Fox

Honey produced by bees that buzz above the alley behind the shop. Tomato sauce made in small batches by the pizza place two doors down. Each of these hipster shopping cart worthy gems can be spied on the shelves of Little Red Fox, a neighborhood cafe, pie-heavy bakery, and market in upper Northwest DC.

"Local is the vision," says Matt Carr who along with his wife, Jena, owns Little Red Fox. "Our motto is we only work with small business." If local is the motto than it's a safe bet that mantra must has something to do with breakfast sandwiches.

"The breakfast sandwich is a big deal for me," says Matt who several days a week still can be found in the kitchen filling morning sandwich orders as well as mixing up batches of homemade hot sauce that accompany many of the offerings. "DC is more of dinner focused town. Part of what we wanted to do here is offer really good breakfast options beyond pastries."

Commitment to breakfast sammies and homestyle cooking runs deep in everything Matt and Jena do at the store. Their allegiance to the neighbors and neighborhood runs equally intense thought their business model. The pair chose to set up shop in DC's Upper Northwest neighborhood because they believed it needed and wanted the kind of fox they were selling. Upon opening 2013 the couple they found their hunch to be true. A line stretched toward the door on day one and the communal farm table near the front window rarely has free seats during peak hours.

The reception from the other independent business on the small stretch of Connecticut Avenue turned out to be even more of a pleasant surprise than the strong customer support. "We are really close with the people at Politics and Prose Bookstore and we are super close with James [Alefantis, the owner of Comet Ping Pong.] We are borrowing stuff from each other's kitchens all the time. [The chef from] Buck's [Fishing and Camping] is here all the time. We share the same customers. It's rare in this business."

This kind of close relationship among and between customers even led to the hiring of the head chef, Bobby Dodd, a classically trained chef who bonded with Matt over their shared love of vinyl. A jazz devotee and audiophile, Dodd brought Matt a Billie Holiday record as a kind of welcome to the neighborhood gift. "I knew I would be a regular so it was my way of introducing myself," Dodd says with a laugh. "And hopefully not looking too creepy."

Months after the exchange when Matt and Jena were looking for a new chef, Dodd become the natural choice. Now that Dodd stands on the other side of the counter, he still extends that personal kind of touch. He takes note and tries to accommodate when regular customers are recovering from surgery or when they can't eat a certain ingredient because of an allergy or an illness. The chef known for his fried chicken recipe also likes to make time to visit with those who frequent the shop like the 83-year-old woman who comes in every Sunday to buy potato salad.

"I know she comes in around four so I try to make some time to hang out with her when I can," he says. "When you have regular customers it's kind of cool to do something special for them. They are more than just customers to me."

5035 Connecticut Ave NW, Washington, DC 20008, (202) 248-6346, littleredfoxdc.com

SWEET POTATO AND FENNEL SOUP

Serves 6–8 people

6 sweet potatoes
1 Spanish, yellow onion
1 fennel (bulb)
1 Granny Smith apple
3 whole allspice berries
1 tablespoon nutmeg (preferably
    freshly ground)
3 each cloves, whole
1 tablespoon thyme (fresh)
Vegetable broth (or water),
    3½ quarts (14 cups)
¼ cup canola oil

SPECIAL EQUIPMENT:
blender, vegetable peeler,
microplane, mesh strainer, large
pot (enough to hold at least two
gallons)

Roughly chop onions, fennel and granny smith apple. Peel and roughly chop sweet potatoes into about 6 pieces per potato. Remove leaves from thyme and set aside.

In a pot, add canola oil, onions, fennel, and apple and allow the vegetables to caramelize. After they begin to brown slightly, add sweet potatoes and vegetable broth.

Using the microplane, zest nutmeg and add to soup.

Add allspice, cloves, and thyme.

Bring to a boil and reduce to simmer until sweet potatoes are soft enough to smash with a fork. Blend the soup until emulsified. Pass through a fine mesh strainer for smooth texture.

Season to taste

Garnish with optional small dice of sweet potato and chopped fennel fronds

BUTTERMILK CHESS PIE

PIE DOUGH:

1½ cups flour
1½ teaspoons salt
1½ teaspoons sugar
4 ounces cold butter cubes
¼ cup cold water

PIE FILLING:

4 eggs
9 ounces sugar
4 ounces buttermilk
2 tablespoons cornstarch
2 tablespoons cornmeal
½ teaspoon salt
1 teaspoon lemon juice
4 ounces butter melted
¼ teaspoon nutmeg
1 cup blueberries

To prepare the pie dough: In a mixer with a paddle attachment, blend flour, salt, and sugar. Add butter and mix on medium-low until butter is combined with some pebble-sized pieces remaining. With mixer on low, stream in cold water until dough just begins to come together. Form dough into a disc and chill for 30 minutes

Roll to fit 9-inch pie shell.

If you are using a glass pie dish, blind bake (pre-bake the crust) for 12 minutes at 350°F and cool before adding the filling.

To prepare the filling: Preheat oven to 350°F. Blend all ingredients together with an immersion blender or whisk until smooth with no lumps. Pour into prepared pie shell. Top with blueberries. Bake 35–45 minutes until the center has a firm jiggle

Allow to cool completely, and chill before serving.

Maketto

James Wozniuk spent hours upon hours deconstructing recipes for Char Siu Pork before building his own. Where the Maketto chef de cuisine lands is with a barbecued Cantonese pork that has about twice as many ingredients as most. Included among the list of co-stars and cameos in his rendering are ginger, hot bean paste, tamari, Shaoxing wine and red rice powder, which is responsible for its distinctive color. The result honors the essence of the original while at the same time producing a remake worthy of a rave review all on its own.

"It's our version of the red cooked pork that you see hanging in windows all over Chinatown," says Wozniuk as he preps the dish as sunlight filters in the open kitchen of Maketto, a Cambodian and Taiwanese restaurant, funky men's shop, bar, bakery, and cafe that operate together in a shared space along H Street. "It has a ton of ingredients but is insanely easy to make. The finished product is amazing. You can serve it in soup, as a sandwich sliced up on bread, or over rice with greens, pickled chilies, and a soy egg."

Wozniuk's red pork most often appears on the H Street restaurant's lunch menu. When combined with rice, the chef likes to refer to the staple as Asian meat and potatoes—comfort food with unlimited flavor possibilities.

Although not found on the ingredient list, time ranks as one of the most important components needed to get this one right. "You need to let it marinade for 12 hours at least," he shares. "If you can get 72 hours you will be super happy."

When Wozniuk needs his own happiness reminder, he glances down at his hand. Gazing up at him is an inked depiction of one of the joyful faces that captivated him when he spent time in Cambodia's Bayon Temple in Angkor.

"All around you see these massive stone statues and they all are smiling," he says of the Khmer temple sometimes called the temple of the smiling gods, which is said to have been built in the 12th or 13th Century. "It's unreal. Wild monkeys are climbing on the statues and when you look out you see that you are in the middle of the jungle. It's insanely beautiful. I put [the face] on my hand so I see it every day and to inspire me to work hard, do well, and get back there."

1351 H St NE, Washington, DC 20002, (202) 838-9972, Maketto1351.com

CHAR SIU PORK

#3 pork shoulder

MARINADE
2 ounces red rice powder
(If you can't find red rice
power you can put red rice
through a coffee grinder to
make your own.)
8 ounces shaoxing wine
8 ounces tamari
8 ounces sweet soy
2 ounces 5 spice
2 ounces garlic (mince)
2 ounces ginger (mince)
4 ounces brown sugar
2 ounces sesame oil
2 ounces hot bean paste
2 ounces tomato paste
2 ounces rice vinegar

GLAZE
4 ounces honey
4 ounces water

Set oven to 300°F. Cut pork lengthwise into 2-inch strips. Combine all marinade ingredients and whisk until well mixed. Add pork. Marinate 24–48 hours turning pork once during this time.

Combine honey and water to make glaze.

Set pork on a roasting rack in the middle of the oven. Roast for 45 minutes. Brush on glaze every 5 minutes for the last 20 minutes.

In warmer weather finish on high grill for a nice charred smoky flavor.

Slice pork and serve over your favorite rice or noodle dish.

Mandu

The Lee family would sit around the kitchen table and roll dumplings the way others would sit around the den and watch reruns. "When I grew up, it was the way we would wind down our day," says Danny Lee, who along with his mother and sister runs the restaurant Mandu, which means "dumpling" in Korean. "That was our family TV night. The same way we fold them now at Mandu is the way we folded them twenty-five years ago in our kitchen."

Danny's mom, Yesoon Lee, was one of those lives-in-the-kitchen women who always loved to entertain and cook. Today, at almost 70, Yesoon continues to do what she loves, putting in many long hours in the back of the house making Korean dishes, some that have been in her family for generations.

One of Yesoon's most requested menu items is her Dolsot Bibim Bap. Danny remembers that when he was growing up, his mom would set out the components of the dish in the kitchen before she went to work so Danny and his sister could put the bibim bap together as an afternoon snack when they came home from school. "The most important part of the dish is the prep," he says. "That's probably true for almost all Korean dishes. Once you do the prep the rest is easy."

The attention to the pre-cooking stages of Mandu's Dolsot Bibim Bap sets it apart from others, Danny says. Each vegetable is prepared and seasoned separately. In order to achieve the authenticity, he recommends investing in stone bowls, which keep the rice dish hot until you reach the bottom.

1805 18th Street NW, Washington, DC 20050, 453 K Street NW, Washington, DC 20001, mandudc.com

DOLSOT BIBIM BAP

Serves 4–6

1 pound beef rib eye
½ cup steamed white rice
1 egg
1½ tablespoons Gochujang
    sauce per bowl of Bibim Bap

MARINADE
    (PER 1 POUND OF BEEF):
¼ cup soy sauce
2 cloves crushed garlic
2 tablespoons sugar
1 tablespoon red wine
1 tablespoon Korean rice syrup

2 stalks chopped green onion
6 tablespoons sesame oil
Ground black pepper to taste
2 teaspoons roasted sesame
    seeds
1½ tablespoons salt
Soybean or vegetable oil
3 tablespoons soy sauce

VEGETABLES:
1 pound fresh spinach
1 pound soybean sprouts
1 pound carrots, peeled
1 pound shiitake mushrooms
1 pound zucchini

To prepare the beef: Combine and mix all the marinade ingredients into a large mixing bowl. Add 1 pound of thinly sliced rib eye and hand-massage the marinade into the beef. Store in refrigerator for at least 2 hours. Remove from refrigerator and massage in 2 tablespoons of sesame oil. Place back in refrigerator for later use.

To prepare the vegetables: Blanch spinach by plunging it into boiling water, then transferring it to a bowl of ice water. Remove from ice bath and lightly press water out. Season with 2 tablespoons sesame oil, 1 teaspoon sesame seeds, and ½ tablespoon salt. Store in refrigerator for later use.

Place sprouts in a pot with 2 cups of water. Once water starts to boil, cover with lid and take off heat and let steam for 5 minutes. Remove from water and season with 2 tablespoons sesame oil, 1 teaspoon sesame seeds, 1 teaspoon salt, and a dash of black pepper. Store in refrigerator for later use.

Cut carrots in half and julienne. Lightly sauté with 1 tablespoon salt and a small amount of soybean or vegetable oil. Let cool and store in refrigerator for later use.

Soak mushrooms for at least 2 hours in water. Strain and julienne. Lightly sauté with 3 tablespoons of thin soy sauce—no oil is needed. Let cool and store in refrigerator for later use.

Cut zucchini in half lengthwise, then thinly slice perpendicular to original cut. Soak in salted water for 10 minutes. Strain water out with cheesecloth, and then lightly sauté in a small amount of soybean or vegetable oil as you did with the carrots. Let cool and store in refrigerator for later use.

To assemble: Scoop ½ cup of steamed white rice into the center of stone bowl, the kind found in most Asian markets.

Place ⅓ cup each of spinach, soybean sprouts, carrots, shiitake mushrooms, and zucchini on top of rice into five equal sections. Take the bowl and black it on a burner range at a high heat.

While the bowl is heating, grill ⅓ cup of the prepared marinated beef by placing thin beef strips on a preheated grill or pan in a single layer. Once cooked and removed from grill, use kitchen shears to cut the strips into small pieces before placing onto the rice.

Lightly dice cooked beef and place it into center of vegetables in the bowl.

Fry one egg sunny-side up and place on top of bowl contents so the yolk is directly in the center.

Quickly drizzle sesame oil along the inner edge of the bowl.

Once rice and oil can be heard steaming, remove from the heat. Place onto wooden bowl holder (again, available at most Asian markets).

Serve with Korean gochujang sauce (a red-bean paste that you can also purchase at most Asian markets).

Food Color

It's a Korean tradition to have five colors—black, white, yellow, green and red—represented in a single dish. Different theories seem to exist on the why of the colorful custom, but most explanations revolve around the belief that each of the five colors represents a sought-after attribute like wisdom (black) or growth (green). Others purport that each color food benefits a different organ in the body, like the heart (red) or the spleen (yellow), or lungs (white). According to the author of the Beyond Kimchee Korean cooking blog (who writes under the penname Holly), each of the colors represents its own matter of universe and meanings. She goes on to explain, "Black belongs to water meaning wisdom of men. White belongs to gold meaning purity. Yellow belongs to soil meaning center of universe (only kings could wear gold color for that reason). Green is wood meaning spring, property. Red belongs to fire meaning creation and passion. A lot of Korean arts and architectures are based on that belief and even the cuisine is influenced by it. That's why you see so many colors in Bibim bap."

Mandu's Dolsot Bibim Bap also uses all five of the significant colors. The black can be found in the stone of the bowl in which it's served. The spinach and zucchini are the green while the sprouts and egg yolks are yellow. The white of the egg fills the white slot and the red comes from the gochujang sauce, a Korean red-bean paste. A perfect rainbow of flavors.

Marcel's

Chef Robert Wiedmaier does not believe in shortcuts, fly-by-night fads, or overnight successes. Instead he subscribes to the school of hard work, attention to the smallest of details, and the cult of blood, sweat, and tears. Wiedmaier is as much about making sure each piece of silver in his dining room sparkles as he is about making certain his kitchen runs with the precision of an army poised for combat. No doubt his ability to see the big and little pictures together at once, along with his fierce passion for this work and his exceptional talent, have allowed him to create one of the city's best and most well-regarded elegant restaurants in town.

The chef extraordinaire also believes in fostering relationships. When talking about the recent farm-to-table trend, he chuckles. "What were they doing before?" asks the chef who worked on farms as a teenager, doing everything from planting corn to slaughtering pigs. "I know every little farm in the area. I've been buying my goat cheese from the same guy for twenty-five years."

This kind of bond extends to almost every aspect of his three local restaurants, including the people who work at Marcel's. "Most of the staff here have all been with me for years," he says. "The maître d' has been here for thirteen years, the chef de cuisine has been with me for fifteen years, most of the waitstaff has been here for ten to thirteen years, and most of the dishwashers for ten years."

2401 Pennsylvania Avenue NW, Washington, DC 20037, (202) 296-1166, marcelsdc.com

BOUDIN BLANC WITH CARAMELIZED ONIONS & BACON LARDONS

Makes 30 Boudins

1 pound boneless, skinless
   chicken breast
8 ounces foie gras
5 ounces squab breast (can
   substitute duck breast)
4¾ cups heavy cream, divided
Salt
3 tablespoons chicken glace
   (chicken stock that has
   been reduced until thick and
   syrupy)
1 tablespoon white truffle oil
2 tablespoons chopped fresh
   black truffles
2 strands hog casings (enough
   for 30 boudins)
8 ounces bacon lardons (cut slab
   bacon into medium dice and
   cook on the stove until crispy)

SAUCE
3 tablespoons unsalted butter,
   divided
1 white onion, diced
½ cup Madeira
1 cup veal stock
Salt, to taste
Pepper, to taste

Grind chicken, foie gras, and squab breast twice through a meat grinder. Transfer ground mixture to a stainless steel bowl and set bowl into another filled with ice.

Pour ½ cup of heavy cream and 1 tablespoon of salt over mixture and put the bowls in refrigerator to chill for 25 minutes.

Remove bowl with meat mixture and incorporate cream with a rubber spatula. Incorporate an additional 4 cups of cream very slowly, whipping with the rubber spatula, adding a dash of salt and then a little cream. Alternate until the 4 cups of cream have been mixed in. Pass mixture through a tamis or fine-mesh strainer and set aside.

In a bowl, combine chicken glace and remaining ¼ cup cream. Incorporate into meat mixture. Add white truffle oil and fresh chopped truffles and combine.

Tie the end of the hog casing. Stuff meat mixture into the casing with a sausage stuffer or pastry bag. Tie the links with butcher's twine to create 2-inch links. Poach sausages in hot salted water until firm, about 15 minutes. Do not let water boil—water should be kept at 175°F.

Plate and spoon sauce (see below) over boudin blanc. Top with bacon lardons.

In a saucepan over medium heat, add 2 tablespoons butter and then the onion. Cook, stirring, until the onion is caramelized, about 5 minutes. Deglaze with Madeira. Add veal stock and 1 tablespoon of butter. Cook over low heat for 5 minutes. Season to taste with salt and pepper.

LAMB TENDERLOINS WRAPPED IN PHYLLO PASTRY WITH BABY CARROTS, CARAMELIZED GARLIC & CUMIN MADEIRA JUS

Serves 6

FOR THE LAMB:

1 tablespoon olive oil for searing the tenderloins

6 lamb tenderloins

1 tablespoon Dijon mustard

6 sheets phyllo pastry

1 cup clarified butter

1 cup fresh spinach, blanched and squeezed

1 cup mushrooms, finely chopped and cooked

FOR THE SAUCE:

3 shallots

1 carrot

1 stalk celery

5 sprigs thyme

½ bottle Madeira

1 cup lamb glace, made from reduced lamb stock

1 cup demiglace, made from reduced veal stock

1 pinch cumin

To prepare the lamb: In a large pan with the olive oil, sear the lamb tenderloins so that they are still rare, about 10 seconds on either side. Cool them down. Cut into thirds and roll in Dijon mustard.

Set out one sheet of the phyllo pastry, brush half with clarified butter, and then fold the pastry in half. Brush the phyllo again, lay two lamb tenderloins down on the phyllo and then put a small amount of spinach in between. Place some mushrooms on top in the middle and spinach on either side of the mushrooms. Top with a third tenderloin, creating a pyramid. Wrap the remaining phyllo around the pyramid, rolling and folding it until it's completely covered. Brush the outside of the roll on all sides. Repeat with the remaining lamb.

To prepare the sauce: Start by chopping the shallots, carrots, and celery. Heat a large saucepot. Lightly sauté the vegetables in olive oil until lightly brown. Add the thyme and Madeira. Reduce the Madeira by two-thirds, then add the lamb glace and demiglace. Reduce until it coats the back of a spoon. Add a hint of cumin, then strain.

To prepare the caramelized garlic: Place 1 cup of peeled garlic cloves into a small sauce pot and fill with water until the cloves are just covered by the water, about 3–4 cups depending on the size of the pot. Bring the water to a boil, then strain the water out of the pot, fill once again with cold water until the cloves are just covered, and bring the water to a boil again. Repeat this series of steps 5 times, keeping the garlic in the water the final round.

In a separate saucepot, place ¼ cup of sugar into the pot and heat on low-medium heat. Swirl the dry sugar regularly until it melts and caramelizes. Once the sugar has turned golden and has melted, add the blanched garlic and half the water [about 1–2 cups] from the pot into the sugar. After you have added the water, the sugar should harden immediately on the bottom of the pot under the garlic. Keeping the pot on low-medium heat, slowly simmer the sugar and garlic mixture until all of the sugar has dissolved into the water, stirring regularly. Some of the water will evaporate as well, creating a thick, syrupy consistency.

To prepare the baby carrots: Place the carrots in a small sauce pot and fill with cold water until the carrots are just covered, about 5–6 cups depending on size of pot. Add the bay leaf, ginger, honey, and salt to the pot. Bring the water to a boil and allow carrots to cook for 3–4 minutes, or until softened. Remove from water and set aside.

Pre-heat oven to 400°F.

To complete and assemble dish: Heat a large pan on top of the stove on high heat. Place the lamb wrapped in phyllo into the pan and sear on all 5 sides for 1–2 minutes per side. Place seared lamb and phyllo onto a baking sheet and place in oven for 5 minutes. Remove the lamb from the oven and allow to rest for 10 minutes. Slice the lamb using a serrated knife into desired portions, and place on plate with the carrots, caramelized garlic, and lamb sauce.

FOR THE CARAMELIZED GARLIC:
6 garlic cloves, peeled
¼ cup sugar

FOR THE CARROTS:
18 baby carrots
1 bay leaf
½ tablespoon ginger root
1 tablespoon honey
1 teaspoon salt

Masseria

A recipe doesn't have to do much to be elevated by the presence of fresh truffles. A dish that can stand tall on its own when you omit the prized delicacy, well, that's another story. Masseria's Linguine with Anchovies, Garlic and Parmigiano is one of those stories.

This traditional pasta treatment often is used in kitchens to showcase the spoils of a truffle harvest. Masseria Owner and Chef Nicholas Stefanelli thought so much of it that he decided to let the recipe stand on its own minus the celebrated ingredient. Diners at the pretty Union Market District restaurant don't seem to be missing a thing.

"I've always loved this dish," says Stefanelli who launched his professional cooking career at Roberto Donna's Galileo and Laboratorio del Galileo. "It's the actual dish we did at Galileo for white truffle season but it's a great dish on its own."

The butter and garlic heavy creation also does not require a tremendous amount of time or an expensive grocery run for those attempting it at home. "You can make it in the time it takes water to boil," says the chef of the Michelin-starred restaurant that celebrates the food of the Puglia region. "And, it just requires staples many people have in the refrigerator – if you are the kind of person who buys anchovies that is."

Stefanelli's linguini recipe isn't the only thing personal the Maryland-native has brought to the restaurant. He grew up eating big family meals with both the Greek and Italian sides of his family and fondly remembers fishing in the Chesapeake Bay for rockfish that would sometimes be cooked up for the gatherings. These experiences continue to influence his menus. A former men's fashion designer, he also picked every tile, surface, and finish for the restaurant and its large patio complete with fire pits, sofas, and candlelight. The whole of the space is as much feast for the eyes as the Masseria approach to cooking is for the palette. Both have been designed to transport diners far away from the industrial setting that, at least for now, surrounds the restaurant. The open kitchen stands as the intentional focus of it all.

"I wanted it to feel like you were walking into my house," says Stefanelli. The first thing someone does is walk into a house is go to the kitchen. It also ensures that the staff has to interact with the guests."

Guests also have the chance unknowingly to interact with the chef's mom. The name of the restaurant, written in her script, graces the menus, chef's coats, and signage. "When it came time to come up with the logo [the consultant] working with him suggested we have friends and family write out the restaurant's name and choose one as the logo," says the chef of the process that led to the handwritten logo in the restaurant's signature shade of aqua blue. "She sent about 30 to me but didn't tell me who wrote them. Without knowing it was hers, I chose my mom's."

1340 4th St NE, Washington, DC 20002, (202) 608-1330, masseria-dc.com

LINGUINE WITH ANCHOVIES, GARLIC & PARMIGIANO

Serves 4

1 pound linguini
4 cloves garlic, thinly sliced
8 anchovies, in olive oil,
    chopped up
¼ pound butter
4 ounces extra virgin olive oil
1 bay leaf
¼ pound Parmigiano-Reggiano,
    grated
1 bunch, small parsley, chopped
Salt to taste
Pepper to taste

Bring a large pot of water to a boil and season with salt. Add the linguini. Stir the pasta every minute or so to make sure it is not clumping together and sticking. In another pot add the oil and butter and let it slowly melt over medium heat. Once the butter is melted add the garlic, anchovy and the bay leaf. Cook the garlic until it is soft and translucent and the anchovy breaks down. Remove the bay leaf and add a ¼ cup of the pasta water to stop the garlic from cooking. Once the linguini has cooked for about 8–9 minutes strain and add it to the anchovy garlic sauce.

Toss it together and finish with parsley pepper and grated Parmigiano-Reggiano.

Matchbox Restaurant

The prospect of attempting homemade pasta tends to rattle the nerves of the less kitchen-confident among us (read: me). But former Chef Shannan Troncoso when she was with Matchbox assured me that two easy-to-find kitchen tools will make this dish—and all pasta-from-scratch endeavors for that matter—a snap. The first item is none other than a basic kitchen scale, which she says should be used in place of measuring cups to measure out the dry ingredients in this recipe. (Troncoso actually recommends using the scale for all baking and dough endeavors.) The second simple-yet-magical piece of equipment in her bag of tricks is a pasta attachment for your mixer. The attachment will eliminate the need for hand cranking, save you time, and overall, cut down on the sweat equity required to create the dish without compromising the final product.

"I bought one for my mom for Christmas and she loves it," Troncoso says of the accessory. She also sent her this recipe for the roasted butternut squash ravioli recipe that the chef makes at Matchbox. Her mom, Shannon tells, also was somewhat apprehensive about attempting the homemade pasta dish. Now with recipe and attachment in hand, she too is a believer.

Troncoso's love of food stretches back to her childhood and her grandmother in southern Georgia, the matriarch of a large Italian family. "I grew up in small town twenty minutes from the border with Florida," says Troncoso, who trained to be a nurse before moving to Denver to go to culinary school. "There were lots of fresh vegetables, fresh food, and farms. In our community and in our family, people would get together every Sunday. I always liked that and I always loved that food was responsible for that."

The former Matchbox chef has another time-saving tip with the squash. Rather than peel it, you can simply have it roast while you prepare the other ingredients. Cut off the top and bottom off of the raw squash, then cut it in half. Scoop out the seeds and let the squash roast at 350°F while getting other ingredients together.

713 H Street NW, Washington, DC 20001, (202) 289-4441, matchbox369.com

HOMEMADE BUTTERNUT SQUASH RAVIOLI

Makes About 120 Ravioli

FOR MUSHROOM CREAM SAUCE:

3 ounces unsalted butter
1 tablespoon minced garlic
½ cup flour
2 cups dry white wine
3 ounces chanterelle mushrooms
1 quart heavy cream
1 cup English peas, shelled
2 tablespoons fresh thyme
    leaves, chopped
2 tablespoons fresh sage leaves,
    chopped
2 tablespoons flat-leaf parsley
    leaves, chopped
1 tablespoon kosher salt
1 teaspoon fresh cracked black
    pepper

FOR PASTA DOUGH:

3½ cups all-purpose flour
5 large eggs
Pinch of kosher salt
1 ounce water (as needed to
    moisten dough)

FOR ROASTED BUTTERNUT SQUASH PUREE:

2–3 whole butternut squash
    (depending on the size)
Extra-virgin olive oil as needed

To prepare the mushroom cream sauce: Melt butter in a heavy-bottom pot over medium heat. Add garlic and cook approximately 1 minute. Whisk in flour to incorporate into the butter and garlic and form a roux. Deglaze with the white wine, using a whisk to mix wine and roux together. Add chanterelle mushrooms and cold heavy cream. Whisk ingredients to break up the roux (this will result in a smooth sauce without lumps). Add remaining ingredients. Whisk sauce until it comes to a boil and becomes thick. Be careful not to burn it!

To prepare the pasta dough using a KitchenAid mixer: Combine flour and eggs in mixer using the paddle attachment. On low speed, add a pinch of salt. Mix for approximately 4 minutes. Slowly add water while dough is mixing. Remove the dough from the bowl and place on a lightly flour-dusted work space. Knead by hand until smooth (approximately 5 minutes). Cover dough with a damp towel and allow to rest for 20 minutes before rolling out.

To prepare the pasta dough by hand: Place flour in a mound on a clean work space. Using your fingers, make a well in the center of the flour. Crack eggs, pinch of salt, and water in a bowl and mix with a fork or whisk. Pour the eggs into the well. Using a fork, gently push the flour into the eggs until combined. Knead dough for approximately 10 minutes until smooth. Cover and allow to rest 20 minutes before rolling out.

To prepare the butternut squash puree: Cut squash in half (I cut off the top and bottom to make them easy to set upright, then slice down the middle). Using a metal spoon, scrape out seeds and coat the squash with olive oil. Place the squash on a parchment paper–lined sheet tray (cookie tray) with the cut side facing down.

Roast in 350°F oven until tender, approximately 25–30 minutes. Cool. Peel off the skin with your fingers. Puree squash in a blender or food processor until smooth.

To prepare the ravioli filling: In a sauté pan, heat olive oil, shallots, sage, and white wine. Cook until tender. Combine with rest of ingredients in a large mixing bowl with a spatula.

To prepare the ravioli: Cut the dough into workable-size pieces. Attach a pasta roller to KitchenAid mixer (or you can use a traditional hand-cranked pasta roller). Using plenty of flour to keep the dough from sticking to the equipment or to itself, feed the dough through the roller, gradually progressing from the thickest setting to the thinnest. The dough will be thin, but not so thin that you can see through it.

Lay the dough on a flour-covered countertop and cut into 4-inch squares (use a pizza cutter, knife, or a square cutting mold).

Place approximately 2 tablespoons of ravioli filling in the center of each square. Brush egg wash on the edges of the ravioli dough and fold in half diagonally to create a triangle. Pinch edges of ravioli tightly. Don't allow any filling to be visible on the edges, or the ravioli will burst when boiling. Place ravioli on a floured plate or tray.

You can freeze the ravioli and they will last for up to 2 weeks. Once the ravioli are frozen, put them in Ziploc freezer bags.

Ravioli and all fresh pasta cook quickly. The ravioli are done once they float in boiling water, approximately 1½ minutes. Once the pasta is done, finish them in the mushroom cream sauce.

To serve: Plate the ravioli while hot. Drizzle with a little hazelnut oil and sprinkle some fresh sage and thyme on top. Enjoy!

FOR RAVIOLI FILLING:
1 ounce extra-virgin olive oil
2 tablespoons minced shallots
2 tablespoons minced fresh sage
2 ounces white wine
4 cups roasted butternut squash puree
1 teaspoon kosher salt
1 teaspoon black pepper
1 pound ricotta cheese
3 tablespoons hazelnut oil

FOR EGG WASH:
1 egg with 1 teaspoon water, beaten well

Miriam's Kitchen

The nonprofit organization Miriam's Kitchen draws inspiration from the Tibetan saying "Compassion is like the moon reflecting on one hundred bowls of water." So it's no wonder the group that feeds and helps thousands each year also named its main fundraiser for the idea wrapped up in those beautiful words. Miriam's Kitchen's annual 100 Bowls of Compassion event raises nearly a quarter of the yearly budget for the group that provides housing, meals, and other services for some of the city's homeless population.

This recipe for salsa verde comes from a recent 100 Bowls of Compassion that had a Road Trip Across America theme. Held at the National Building Museum, the event featured dishes inspired by the hometown memories of both the guests served at Miriam's Kitchen and the volunteer sous chefs who help create healthy, from-scratch meals every day for those guests. The extensive gourmet menu was made entirely by skilled Miriam's Kitchen volunteers with in-kind donations, allowing an impressive 90 percent of the ticket cost to go directly to supporting the group's homeless guests.

"Recipes like this one (featured at our New Mexico table) highlight the diverse regions of our country," explains Former Director of Kitchen Operations Chef Steve Badt. "With a peppery bite and a bright acid contrast, this salsa is mild, but can be made spicier by substituting Anaheim chilies for the poblano peppers."

Each day donations of food from local markets, farmers, hunters, fishers, and others get delivered to Miriam's Kitchen and determine what will be created that day. Two professional cooks, along with a steady flow of dedicated volunteers, turn the ingredients into healthy, homemade dishes that they serve to the homeless individuals who come to Miriam's

Kitchen to eat and receive other services like legal help or free Metro cards. Volunteers do everything from peeling carrots to scrubbing pots to serving food. No kitchen experience is needed to help out at Miriam's Kitchen, just a good attitude and a commitment to volunteering at least once a month. The payoff can be seen reflected in the faces of both the guests and the volunteers.

2401 Virginia Avenue NW, Washington, DC 20037, (202) 452-8926, miriamskitchen.org

CHARRED POBLANO SALSA VERDE

Serves 6

1 large onion
2 poblano peppers
1 jalapeño pepper
Kosher salt to taste
½ cup grape-seed oil or olive oil
  (a mild olive oil, pure rather
  than extra-virgin, which is too
  grassy and bitter) plus extra
  for coating vegetables
3½ tablespoons apple cider
  vinegar
Freshly ground black pepper to
  taste

Heat a heavy-bottom cast-iron pan until it is very hot. Slice the onions into thick rings. Season onions and whole peppers with salt and enough oil to cover evenly and place peppers in the pan in one layer. Roast on all sides until they turn black or a deep golden brown. Don't be afraid to leave them in the pan a little longer than you think you should, but don't let the peppers turn white—this is a sign they are completely burned through. Sear the onions on both sides until they are slightly black or a deep golden brown color.

Place peppers and onions in a bowl and keep covered with tight-fitting plastic wrap. Leave bowl on the countertop, not in the fridge. This allows the peppers and onions to steam until they are soft to the touch, about 10–12 minutes.

Peel, seed, and chop the peppers. Finely chop the onions and add to the peppers.

Add the oil and vinegar to the vegetables. Mix thoroughly. Add salt and pepper lightly, then taste and adjust if necessary.

Mitsitam Native Foods Cafe

As a kid, Freddie Bitsoie remembers white teachers organizing games of telephone to demonstrate the "unreliability" of oral traditions like those of his family and ancestors. Even then Bitsoie, a member of the Navajo Nation, didn't buy it.

"At the end of the game the teachers would say 'see how the story always changes because it has been passed down,'" tells the executive chef of the Mitsitam Native Foods Cafe housed in the National Museum of the American Indian in Washington, DC, who grew up in the Southwest living both on and off the reservation. "'See how you probably don't know your real story.' It was a way of looking at the people who lived years ago and making them seem stupid."

Today the Mitsitam Native Foods Cafe's first Native chef, proudly and reliably tells those real stories each and every day through the food he creates at the cafe in National Museum of the American Indian. "The only difference between Native cuisine and others is that it hasn't been codified," Bitsoie tells.

The chef is hoping to do his part to change that by using his food to helps others better understand dishes with ancient, smart, and proud histories that he hopes to help take further out of the culinary margins. His Arizona posole recipe is one of those dishes.

A hominy based stew, posole is an ancient dish and the oldest continually made dish in history, according to Bitsoie, a classically trained chef who also has studies anthropology, archeology, and art history. He goes on to explain that the Natives who first made the dish thousands of years ago figured out a way of cooking it like this to get the most protein possible from the corn. The red color of the corn-based dish—from the tomatoes that help cut the spice—is one of the ingredients that make it specific to Arizona.

Like Butter: Julia Child's Kitchen at the Smithsonian

Just a short walk from the Mitsitam Cafe, museum visitors with a foodie side can drool over Julia Child's actual kitchen from her Cambridge home housed at the nearby Smithsonian's National Museum of American History. The room, which served as the backdrop for several of her popular television cooking programs, is a necessary pilgrimage for anyone who owns a dog-eared copy of Child's best-selling *Mastering the Art of French Cooking* and is worth the trip for anyone else who might get a kick out of a true mid-century kitchen.

Highlights include the mortar and pestle the chef purchased in Paris while studying at the Cordon Bleu, the straight razor she used to slash the tops of French bread, and her beloved "Big Garland," the six-burner Model 182 Garland commercial stove she purchased secondhand in 1956. (Child used an electric wall oven, which also is part of the kitchen exhibit, when she cooked on TV, but she always preferred her Garland.)

If you stand very still you can almost hear the onions browning in butter and smell the beef bourguignon simmering on top of the Big Garland.

"Color is very important to food," he says. "In Native American cuisine we have purple food and blue food – colors we are not accustom to seeing in other cuisines."

When Bitsoie at the museum in 2016 after working at the restaurant at a Native American casino, the chef decided to keep fry bread on the menu. While he obviously has issues with the why it had to come to be he says he does not have issue with fry bread itself.

"I eat it, I like it, I make it," he says. "The federal government gave us flour, baking powder, salt and sugar we had to find a way to it eat it."

"No one should be ashamed of what they are eating," he adds.

Fry bread, which was on the menu at the cafe since it opened, follows a simple recipe and comes with a complex history. The deep-fried flat bread first came into being on the reservations. It used ingredients like sugar, white flour, and other controversial foods that were introduced by the US government and other outside sources and not previously part of the Native American diet. Yet at the same time fry bread is an almost ubiquitous part of the Native American food culture and found in many a Native American home, with each family often having its own subtle take on the basic formula.

"I compare it to how everyone's grandmother has a meat loaf recipe," says Chef Richard Hetzler, the first chef to head up the kitchen at Mitsitam Native Foods Cafe, housed in the Smithsonian National Museum of the American Indian on the Mall.

"Everyone makes it a little bit different. It's a recipe that is hard to mess up."

The team at the popular museum cafe make about two thousand pieces a day. Hetzler recommends topping the fry bread with ground beef and says that those who wish to avoid the deep-frying can try brushing the bread with olive oil and grilling it. The classically trained chef, who has fostered a deep respect for what he says are the native roots of most food traditions, sometimes can't believe the success of the Mitsitam Cafe, which he helped launch in 2003 after immersing himself in anything he could get his hands on about native cuisine and culture. It was something of a risky experiment, launching such a specialized cafeteria on the Mall. All these years later, many consider the cafe, which features food from five different regions, a bigger draw than the museum itself.

"Right before we opened I thought, in six months we'll be serving burgers, pizza, and hot dogs," he says. "Now people like to say that we are a cafe with a museum."

Smithsonian National Museum of the American Indian, 4th Street and Independence Avenue SW, Washington, DC 20560, (202) 633-6644, mitsitamcafe.com

EASY WINTER POSOLE BY CHEF FREDDIE BITSOIE

Serves 4

3 tablespoons olive oil
1 pound pork butt, cut into
    medium-size dice
Salt and pepper to taste
1 medium onion, diced small
3 cloves garlic, minced
5 sprigs thyme
2 bay leaves
2 tablespoons tomato paste
3 tablespoons paprika
3 tablespoons chili powder
1 teaspoon cumin
1 teaspoon coriander
1 14-ounce can diced tomatoes
28 ounces cooked hominy
32 ounces chicken stock
Cilantro, chopped, for garnish
Thyme, for garnish

In a large, heavy-bottomed pot, heat the olive oil. Sear the diced pork in the oil, adding salt and pepper to taste. Remove pork from pot when all sides are seared.

Add to pot the diced onion, minced garlic, thyme sprigs and bay leaves. Sweat the ingredients for about 7 minutes, or until onions are translucent.

Add the tomato paste, paprika, chili powder, cumin and coriander, and allow these ingredients to toast. Add the diced tomatoes.

Add the seared pork back into the pot, along with the cooked hominy. Stir all ingredients together well and then add the chicken stock. Only add enough stock to just cover the ingredients.

Bring posole to a boil, then reduce heat to a simmer. Allow to simmer uncovered for about 20 minutes as the liquid reduces and the posole develops the consistency of a stew. Adjust seasonings to taste.

To serve, ladle posole into bowls and garnish with cilantro and thyme.

FRY BREAD
RECIPE BY CHEF RICHARD HETZLER

Makes 6 Round Flat Breads

2 cups all-purpose flour
1 teaspoon baking powder
1 teaspoon salt
2 tablespoons sugar
¾ cup milk, plus more if
    necessary
Corn or canola oil for deep frying
Sugar mixed with ground
    cinnamon for topping
    (optional)

SPECIAL EQUIPMENT:
Deep-fat thermometer

In a medium bowl, combine the flour, baking powder, salt, and sugar. Stir with a whisk to blend. Mix in the milk to make a stiff dough, adding a bit more milk if necessary. On a lightly floured board, divide the dough into 6 pieces. Form each into a ball, and then roll into disks about ¼-inch thick.

In a Dutch oven or deep fryer, heat 3 inches of oil to 350°F on a deep-fat thermometer. Using a sharp knife, cut an X in the center of each dough disk. Place one disk at a time in the hot oil and cook until golden brown (about 2 minutes) on each side. Using tongs, transfer to a paper towel–lined plate to drain. Keep warm in an oven set to a low temperature while frying the remaining disks.

Serve at once, either plain or sprinkled with cinnamon sugar.

Pizzeria Orso

Former Pizzeria Orso chef, Will Artley believes in the art and humor of making good pizza. The humor is all his own but the artistry comes from intense study with a master pizzailo from the Associazione Vera Pizza Napoletana, a non-profit organization devoted to promoting and protecting "true Neapolitan pizza." The only group of its kind, the VPN certifies pizzailos after they successfully complete a rigorous training in the age-old craft of Neapolitan pizza making and have determined that the individual can perform to the group's high standards. His Thunder Kat meets the VPN's strict criteria for Neapolitan pizza only when cooked in a wood-burning oven—one of the VPN requirements—like the one at Orso but it still tastes delicious when made at home in a conventional oven.

"I am a certified pizzailo from the VPN and also certified in Artisan breads," he tells. "My pizza training was under President of VPN Americas Peppe Miele and master teacher José Barrios."

Artley began cooking long before he ever got his pizza certification. When he was growing up, his mom taught him to make an array of traditional Mexican dishes and from that his love of being in the kitchen was born. He went on to study and graduate from the Culinary Institute of America and worked in many types of restaurants before entering the wonderful world of pizza when he took over the kitchen at Pizzeria Orso in Falls Church. "Today I find my inspiration in local food, my life partner Kimberly, and our four dogs—Levi, Raiyna, Chip, and Todd," he happily tells. Chef Artley no longer is with Orso but his Thunder Kat Pie still meets VPN strict standards.

400 South Maple Avenue, Falls Church, VA 22046, (703) 226-3460, pizzeriaorso.com

THE THUNDER KAT PIE

Makes 1

PIZZA DOUGH:

1 cup room temperature water
1 teaspoon salt
3 cups 00 flour ("00" is a classification used in Italy to tell how fine a flour is ground. The 00 flour is highly refined and has the consistency of soft powder.)
½ cup sour starter
2 tablespoons olive oil

SAUCE:

1 can of San Marzano tomatoes (Artley, with a smile, holds that there is no replacement for this)
2 teaspoons sea salt

TOPPINGS:

5 ounces salami
4 ounces pepperoni
3 buffala or regular mozzarella
5 each grilled Fresno peppers sliced thinly

To prepare the pizza dough: Combine half the water and salt in a bowl and mix for 2 minutes on the lowest speed. Add half the flour and continue on speed 1 of your mixer with the dough hook for another 2 minute then add starter and mix for 1 minute. Add everything else and mix for 14 minutes. Place the mixed dough in a lightly oiled mixing bowl and allow it to ferment for 3 hours. After three hours it should spring back half way to the touch. At this point you can weigh your dough balls out to 8 ounces and allow it to rest for one more hour.

To prepare the sauce: Hand chop the tomatoes after they are drained (save the liquid). Combine tomatoes and sea salt. Yes, that's it. It's all about the tomatoes.

To assemble: After the dough has rested for an hour, use a rolling pin to roll it out to desired size.

Use a 1-inch rim around the outside of the dough, which will make for a nice sized crust. Assemble the pizza on top of an upside down cookie tray with a light dusting of cornmeal, which allows you to slide the pizza right onto the stone.

Using a large spoon or 2-ounce ladle, spoon the sauce on to the middle of the dough. Keeping the spoon against the dough, use a circular motion to spread the sauce over the dough. Do this until the sauce is lightly spread throughout, stopping an inch before the edge of the pizza dough. Make sure not to spread the sauce all the way to the edge, leave yourself an inch. (If you spread the sauce all the way to the end you will not be able to stretch it without getting your fingers in the sauce and the crust will get weighed down.)

Start by placing the salami first and try to make sure each bite will get just enough. Then follow with the pepperoni, the cheese, and finally the Fresno peppers. Remember with this pizza less is more—too many topping will weigh down your dough and make for a lot of sogginess.

Turn on your oven (with pizza stone in it) as high as it will go, allowing it to preheat for 15 minutes.

Rotate the pizza every 4 minutes until the crust become golden brown.

To serve: When it's done, remove the pizza from the oven and allow it to rest for 4 minutes—the pizza is still cooking during this time. Allow the pizza to cook, slice and serve.

Bar Manager Adam Bernbach comes to spirits by way of coffee. As a high school student at the Edmund Burke School, he got a job as a roaster at the nearby Sirius Coffee Company, which once stood above the Van Ness Metro station. Working at the indie shop opened up his palate and his imagination. "I had to taste everything and I got very into the flavors in food," says the mixologist who heads up the bar program at Proof. Estadio, 2 birds 1 stone, and doi moi. "Over time, through coffee I got into single-malt scotch, and through scotch I got into other spirits, and through spirits I got into cocktails."

Much to his delight, Bernbach has watched the cocktail scene in DC soar. "There's been a real explosion of the cocktail scene here, especially in the past five years," he says. "It's phenomenal. People's tastes are getting more sophisticated."

Customers, he finds, are now more willing to try new combinations and ingredients, a development that has fostered the opportunity for more creativity when it comes to experimenting behind the bar. His "Root" drink on the menu at Proof is a good example of how he puts new spins on classic concoctions. Named for its earthy ingredients and his late mother (whose name was Ruth, which in Hebrew is pronounced, "Rut"), the signature drink combines El Tesoro blanco tequila, Ramos Pinto white port, and Chartreuse. It's finished off with a touch of citrus and served in a coupe glass.

775 G Street NW, Washington, DC 20001, (202) 737-7663, proofdc.com

ROOT COCKTAIL

Makes 1 Cocktail

1½ ounces blanco tequila
½ ounce Chartreuse
1 ounce white port
Orange zest

To create the cocktail, pour ingredients one at a time over ice and stir well.

Strain the mixture into a coupe glass and garnish with an orange zest.

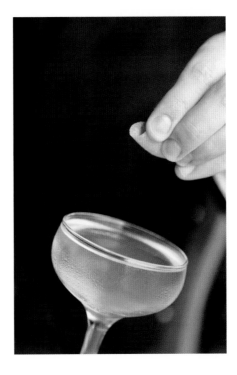

Quill

Calling Quill a hotel bar is like saying the Constitution is a just another legal document or the White House is one more home office. From the moment the top hat–clad doorman ushers you into the historic Beaux Arts hotel, it becomes apparent that you have not arrived just anywhere for a nightcap. The historic boutique hotel stands on 16th Street, just blocks away from the White House, and the clientele who come to Quill reflect the boutique hotel's stately location. Local power players as well as high-profile guests can sometimes be spotted sipping at Quill, engaged in what appears to be intriguing inside-the-Beltway banter, or just soaking up the cocktail culture.

Behind the bar itself, the skilled staff elevates Quill cocktail preparation to an art form. All the mixers here are house-made and expertly blended with herb-infused alcohols. Kentucky Salty Dog remains a Quill favorite and serves as something of its signature cocktail, expertly showing how the bar prides itself on reimagining classic combinations. If you come in an adventurous mood, consider ordering the "Master Mind," and the mixologist will create a "spontaneous" cocktail just for you.

As an homage to the hotel's presidential namesake, Quill's striking interior is steeped in Jeffersonian images and lore. The eighteenth-century European maps that adorn the walls trace the actual routes the author of the Declaration of Independence took when he traveled through the wine regions of France, Germany, and Italy. Under foot, the parquet flooring recreates the pattern Jefferson, who was also a skilled architect, designed for Monticello's main salon.

The Jefferson, 1200 16th Street NW, Washington, DC 20036, (202) 448-2300, jeffersondc.com

KENTUCKY SALTY DOG COCKTAIL

Makes 1 Cocktail

3 grapefruit wedges
2 ounces Bulleit bourbon
1½ teaspoons Aperol
1½ teaspoons grapefruit bitters
1½ teaspoons simple syrup

Add grapefruit wedges and bourbon to shaker and muddle. Add Aperol, bitters, and simple syrup, and shake vigorously. Strain into a salted rocks glass.

Rasika West End

Chef Vikram Sunderam playfully calls his Avocado Banana Chaat "Indian guacamole." The award-winning Rasika chef uses many of the same ingredients in his version as those typically found in guacamole and he even created his Avocado Banana Chaat to be enjoyed in much the same way as its Mexican cousin—served cold and at the start of the meal. The result is a dish that artfully blends authentic Indian flavors with modern tastes.

Chaat is something of a generic term used to describe a whole range of popular savory snacks in India often sold from street carts in the cities and on the beaches. "Chaat is a very traditional way of cooking," says Sunderam. "It means savories. The basic chaat is a bit sweet, a bit tangy, and a bit spicy. We have potato chaat, fruit chaat, chicken chaat, so I thought why not have an avocado chaat."

The first step in this recipe happens not in the kitchen but at the farmers' market or produce aisle, when you go to pick out the avocados. Look for ripe, firm avocados with only a slight amount of give. If they are too soft, the recipe won't turn out as well. Grilling the banana, rather than using it uncooked, adds another level of texture that complements the avocados and other enticing flavors in this chaat.

While Sunderam includes a chutney recipe—and a wonderful one at that—he does say that you can substitute a store-bought one if you are short on time. If you do decide to make the chutney, you can keep it in the refrigerator for a week or two.

1190 New Hampshire Avenue, NW, Washington, DC 20037, (202) 466-2500, rasikarestaurant .com/westend

AVOCADO BANANA CHAAT

Serves 4

FOR THE TAMARIND CHUTNEY:
4 ounces pound tamarind
2 ounces dates
1 teaspoon freshly grated ginger
2 garlic cloves
½ ounce jaggery (a pure,
    unrefined, whole sugar)
2 tablespoons sugar
2 whole red chilies
2 bay leaves
½ teaspoon fennel seeds
¼ teaspoon roasted cumin
    powder
¼ teaspoon red chili powder
¼ teaspoon black salt
Salt to taste

2 ripe but firm avocados
½ cup chopped onions
½ cup chopped tomatoes
1 teaspoon roasted cumin
    powder
½ teaspoon red chili powder
¼ teaspoon black salt
4 tablespoons tamarind chutney
2 ripe but firm bananas
2 tablespoons chopped fresh
    cilantro
Black pepper to taste

To prepare the tamarind chutney: Put all the ingredients except cumin, chili powder, and salts in a heavy-bottom pan. Add enough water to cover the ingredients. Let the mixture boil and then simmer till the dates and tamarind are soft and mashed. Pass the mixture through a fine strainer. Season the extract with the roasted cumin powder, red chili powder, black salt, and salt. Cool and keep aside.

Use 4 tablespoons for the recipe and keep the rest refrigerated.

To assemble: Cut the avocado into quarter-inch dice. Add the rest of the ingredients, except the bananas and cilantro, in a bowl and mix well. Mix in 4 tablespoons of tamarind chutney.

Cut the banana in half and then cut lengthwise and grill on a skillet. Season with salt and black pepper.

Arrange the banana on top of the avocado and garnish with chopped fresh cilantro. Serve cold.

Red Hook Lobster Pound Food Truck

True story. A woman once passed out when she finally got up to the window at the Red Hook Lobster Pound truck. Thankfully she came to in time to order and eat her lobster roll. Such is the power of the lobstah.

One of the city's most popular and at times faint-inducing food trucks brings the taste of Maine to DC by way of Brooklyn. There, Susan Povich and her husband Ralph Gorman came up with the idea to drive up to Maine, fill a truck with lobsters, and sell them back in New York at an empty storefront. Hundreds of pounds went in hours. After a while she started making lobster rolls that sold at flea markets with equal fervor. At that point she asked her Washington-based cousin, Doug Povich, if he wanted to bring the business down here. Doug, teamed up with his friend, the Culinary Institute of America graduate Leland Morris, and a food truck was born.

"Every summer my family would go up to Maine," says Doug, a telecom lawyer, proving once again that everyone in DC is really a lawyer. "We'd have lobster rolls every day. Sometimes twice a day. Our roll is a distillation of what we thought were all the best lobster rolls we would have up in Maine."

The recipe for the roll that sometimes commands a line two hundred people long is a well-guarded secret, but part of the appeal, Doug reveals, is in the mayo. Red Hook uses house-made mayo that Susan makes up in New York. "It's lemon-based and very light," he tells.

While you have to queue up to get the real deal from the truck, Red Hook's recipe for steamed whole lobster is a good start for those who want to try and re-create the magic at home. One lobster will do if you make it at home, but think about this. The truck goes through thousands of pounds of lobster meat every week (they bring them down about two or three times a week) and it takes about eight lobsters to get one pound of meat, a statistic that could make anybody a bit weak in the knees.

@LobstertruckDC, redhooklobsterdc.com

LOBSTER ON THE GRILL

Serves 4

4 live Maine lobsters, 1½–2
  pounds each
4 cloves fresh garlic
10 sprigs of thyme
4 lemons
1½ pounds salted butter, cut into
  cubes
Coarse sea salt to taste
1 cup dry white wine
4 sheets heavy-duty aluminum
  foil

Fire up your grill. The lobster truckers prefer using a natural lump, hardwood charcoal. You want the high flames to subside, leaving a nice, hot bed of burning coals.

Kill the lobsters by placing the tip of a chef's knife about 2 inches back from the eyes on the top of the head of the lobster and driving the knife down through the head until it hits the cutting board. The blade of the knife should be facing the eyes and the bolster of the knife should be pointed toward the tail. Roll the blade of the knife down so that the blade cuts between the eyes and through the shell completely.

After killing the lobsters, place them back in the fridge for about 15 minutes.

Prepare your garlic by smashing the cloves with your knife and removing the outer skin. Then mince the garlic.

Prepare your thyme by pulling the leaves from the stems. Give the thyme a rough chop. Mix the chopped garlic and thyme together.

Cut your lemons in half and set to the side.

Remove the lobsters from the fridge and prepare them for grilling. Take each lobster and hold it with its belly facing up. Using a chef's knife, cut the lobster lengthwise from head to tail, cutting through the body, meat, and through the back shell. It helps to start by placing the tip of the knife where the tail meets the body and rolling the blade down to cut the tail in half (lengthwise) first. Then reverse the motion and cut the body and head in half.

Remove the tomalley and any roe and reserve for other recipes, or discard it.

Remove the rubber bands from the claws.

Place each half lobster on a sheet of foil, belly up.

Place a few cubes of butter down the length of the lobster, being sure to cover the tail. Sprinkle the fresh garlic, thyme, and sea salt down the length of the lobster.

Sprinkle the wine down the length of the lobster.

Wrap the lobsters individually in the foil sheets. The wrap should be tight with closed ends, so the ingredients stay in the foil and on the lobster. Place the wrapped lobsters on the grill, belly-side up, for about 9–12 minutes.

Place remaining butter in a small pot and place on the side of your grill to melt.

Dip the cut side of each half lemon in butter and place, cut side down, on the grill.

Remove the lobsters from the foil and turn belly-side down, and grill for an additional 3–5 minutes. Try to keep the melted butter and other liquids released during cooking in the foil instead of falling on the burning coals. This will help prevent a flare-up and the resulting soot from getting on the lobster. You want to finish cooking the meat and get some nice grill marks on the flesh of the tail. You also want to caramelize the garlic and thyme.

The lobsters are finished cooking when the meat is opaque. Adjust your grilling time after you remove the lobster from the foil, if necessary. Larger lobsters will require more time. Also, large claws require more cooking time. Adjust by moving the tail portion of the lobster off the center of the grill for less direct heat with the claws over more direct heat.

Check your lemons. Pull them off the grill when nicely browned on the cut side. You do not need to flip your lemons.

Let the lobsters rest for 5 minutes before eating.

Pour the melted butter in a bowl.

Arrange the grilled lobsters and lemons on a platter.

Enjoy with friends and a cold root beer!

Remember, have fun! Try this recipe with your favorite herbs and flavorings. In our opinion, lobster is best when prepared simply allowing the natural flavor of the lobster to shine through.

Ripple

Chef Logan Cox is one of a growing number of chefs worldwide embracing the practice of hyper-local wild foraging. "Most mornings I wake up an hour earlier than I need to and forage," explains the Petworth resident. "Some days I go down to Rock Creek Park where it's more lush, but once you know what you are looking for you start to see it everywhere."

And, he does mean everywhere. Cox has collected food everywhere from cracks in the sidewalk to the side of the road. Wild dandelions, ramps, and different sorrels are some of the ingredients Cox finds in these and other places around town to bring back to the Ripple kitchen. The pine needles he uses in this recipe to smoke the arctic char fillets typically come from Ordway Street right around the corner from Ripple. Cox, who cites the book Stalking the Wild Asparagus as one of his inspirations, calls foraging the ultimate locavore moment. "Food," he adds, "really is everywhere."

If you want to attempt smoking the fillets with the aroma of the pine needles, the first step is to soak them in warm water overnight, tells the chef who started college on a football scholarship and plays the bass. You can create a makeshift smoker, if you don't own one, by using deep metal pans, placing one inside another. If you can't find pine needles, rosemary works as a substitute.

Chef Logan Cox closed Ripple and left DC for the Pacific Northwest. His approach to the menu has been built upon by the new Ripple team.

RED RUSSIAN KALE SALAD, ANCHOVY DRESSING, TOASTED COUSCOUS, PICKLED POTATOES & SMOKED ARCTIC CHAR RILLETTES

Serves 6

FOR THE ANCHOVY DRESSING:
5 egg yolks
1 egg
Juice of two lemons
Juice of two limes
5 anchovy fillets
7 garlic cloves, peeled and finely
    chopped
¼ pound Parmesan cheese,
    finely grated
7 ounces of olive oil
3½ ounces finely diced red onion
2½ ounces finely chopped chives
2½ ounces yellow mustard seed
Pinch of salt, to taste

FOR THE SMOKED ARCTIC CHAR
    RILLETTES:
1 handful of pine needles
1 bunch sage
3 sprigs rosemary
2 fillets artic char
1 cup crème fraîche
Pinch of chives
2 teaspoons kosher salt

To prepare the anchovy dressing: In a blender combine the yolks, egg, lemon and lime juices, anchovies, garlic, and Parmesan. Blend till smooth. While blender is still running, slowly drizzle in the olive oil until dressing is thick, creamy and emulsified. Pour the dressing into a bowl and mix in the remaining ingredients.

To prepare the arctic char rillettes: Add pine needles, sage, and rosemary to a smoker. Place arctic char fillets over smoking herbs and needles until fully cooked. This is known as a "hard smoke," meaning that the temperature of the smoke needs to be high enough to also cook the fish completely. The smoking process should only take around 6 minutes.

Reserve char and let rest to room temperature.

Add room temperature char, crème fraîche, chives, and salt to a KitchenAid mixer bowl with the paddle attachment. Paddle the mixture on medium speed until well incorporated. The mixture should be spreadable, or have the consistency of rillettes or resemble a nicely textured puree.

To prepare the couscous: In a 350°F oven toast the couscous by itself on a sheet pan till golden brown. Remove from oven and let sit until room temperature.

In a small saucepan bring salt, water, and olive oil to a boil. Add the toasted couscous to the boiling water, immediately turn the heat down to low, and cover with a lid. The couscous should be ready in 12–15 minutes. Reserve and chill.

To prepare the pickled potatoes: Remove sliced fingerling potatoes from rinsing water, place in a bowl big enough to hold the potatoes, and the hot pickling liquid. In a small sauce pot bring vinegar, water, salt, bay leaves, mustard seed, and cloves to a boil. Once liquid is boiling, pour over top of the fingerling potatoes. Chill potatoes in the pickling brine over night to completely infuse the brine.

To plate: In a small bowl add a spoonful of dressing to a salad bowl, gently toss the kale to evenly coat the greens. (It's always best to start with too little dressing; you can always add more if desired.) Add the couscous and pickled potatoes to the same bowl and mix gently for even distribution.

On a plate place a long smear of Smoked Artic Char Rillette with an off set spatula or spoon. Using the smear as a guide, gently place the now dressed salad in a line next to the rillette being sure to leave the rillette exposed.

FOR THE COUSCOUS:
1 cup Israeli couscous
2 teaspoons kosher salt
1½ cups water
1 teaspoon of olive oil

FOR PICKLED POTATOES:
10 fingerling potatoes, thinly
    sliced ¼ inch thick on a
    mandoline and rinsed of
    excessive starch
3½ ounces white wine vinegar
10½ ounces water
¾ ounce of kosher salt
2 bay leaves
⅓ ounce mustard seed
4 whole cloves

1 head Red Russian kale,
    washed and removed of
    fibrous stems

COMPOSED SEASONAL VEGETABLE SALAD, GOAT YOGURT, CARDAMOM & CHARRED LETTUCE PUREE

Serves 6

This is a salad that we have on our menu at Ripple every day. We purchase 95 percent of our produce from surrounding organic farmers, growers, and foragers. This dish allows us to showcase all the great things our area has to offer, sometimes found directly in our backyards. The treatment of the vegetables is based on how the vegetable is that day—some are roasted, others blanched, others braised, some pickled, and others served raw. The preparations change daily.

To prepare the charred lettuce puree: In a 400°F oven place the leek tops, greens, stems, and vegetable tops on a sheet tray. Roast in oven till all items are black, charred, and brittle. You cannot overcook this—the idea is to essentially burn the vegetables.

In a small saucepan, place the onion, water, butter, and salt and simmer until the onions are meltingly tender. Remove from heat.

Place the stewed onions in the blender with the charred vegetables, puree until smooth and spreadable, season with salt to taste. Chill.

To prepare the cardamom vinaigrette: In a small sauce pan add the red wine vinegar and cardamom pods, reduce by half. Remove from heat and let chill to room temperature. Place cooked vinegar in a mixing bowl and whisk in olive oil. Season with salt to taste. Reserve.

To plate: On a plate, place a smear of the charred lettuce puree off to the side with an offset spatula. In a small salad bowl add the cardamom vinaigrette and one portion of the vegetables with a pinch of salt, coat evenly. Decoratively place the vegetables in a natural fashion. Place goat yogurt in a squeeze bottle and place small dots in and around the vegetables. Garnish the now-plated vegetables with decorative greens and herbs such as nasturtium, baby dandelion, chickweed, fennel fronds, lemon balm, pea shoots, and purslane.

FOR THE CHARRED LETTUCE PUREE:
Handful of leek tops
½ pound salad or other greens
½ pound vegetable stems and tops
1 yellow onion, julienned
1 cup water
4 tablespoons unsalted butter
Salt to taste

FOR THE CARDAMOM VINAIGRETTE:
½ cup red wine vinegar
10 cardamom pods, smashed to expose the interior seeds
1⅓ cups olive oil
Salt to taste
¼ cup goat yogurt in a squeeze bottle
2 sprigs nasturtium (optional)
2 sprigs baby dandelion (optional)
2 sprigs chickweed (optional)
2 sprigs fennel fronds (optional)
2 sprigs lemon balm (optional)
2 sprigs pea shoots (optional)
2 sprigs purslane (optional)

GLUTEN-FREE CHOCOLATE FINANCIER

Makes 12–16 Mini Muffins

6 ounces (1½ sticks) butter

4 ounces dark chocolate (70 percent), melted

2 cups ground almond flour

6 tablespoons cocoa powder

¼ teaspoon salt

1½ cups confectioners' sugar

5 ounces white chocolate pieces, finely chopped

5 egg whites

Preheat the oven to 325°F. Brown the butter in pot by melting over a medium heat and continuing to let it cook until there is a very nutty aroma and the butter has become light brown in color. Set aside.

Melt chocolate over a double boiler. Set aside.

Mix almond flour, cocoa powder, salt, sugar, and white chocolate pieces in bowl of mixer with a paddle attachment.

Add egg whites, chocolate, and butter slowly to bowl and mix until combined.

Scoop your batter into desired molds (a mini cupcake pan works best). Bake for about 15–20 minutes, or until a skewer comes out clean.

RIS

Ris Lacoste speaks the way she cooks: with kindness, warm details, and without the slightest hint of pretense.

The chef and owner of this West End restaurant approaches the business with a studied but gentle touch and a passion for feeding others that was passed on by her mother. "There were seven of us and my father and we had three hot meals a day," says Lacoste, who was born Doris but hasn't been called that in many years. "We ate at five o'clock every single day and my mother made everything."

One of the most beloved dishes of many well-loved dishes back in the day in the Lacoste family was her mom's Chicken Pot Pie, which now graces the menu at her restaurant. "My mom used to make it in a Pyrex baking dish and would line it with her own pie crust that she made with lard. We would fight over crust leftover in the bottom of the dish."

Lacoste has tweaked the savory pie slightly from her mother's version, but the soul of the dish remains intact. When making this wonderfully comforting family recipe at home, Lacoste stresses the importance of cooking the filling and crust together at the same time. "It's crucial to bake the pastry with the filing," she says. "The crust and filling have to talk to each other."

Although Lacoste enjoyed being in her mom's kitchen and worked at a butcher shop and restaurants throughout high school and college, her career path in cooking didn't take shape until after graduation. She began her studies at the University of Rochester as pre-med but ultimately graduated with a degree in French from the University of California at Berkeley. From there she went to Paris with the idea of becoming a translator for the UN. A series of serendipitous twists and turns led her to enroll at the Anne Willan's La Varenne École de

Cuisine, and thus began her storied culinary career, which began in France. There she met greats like Julia Child (years later she had the honor of preparing dinner for Child on her 90th birthday) and in time Lacoste landed on L Street at the pretty, light-filled restaurant that bears her name.

2275 L Street NW, Washington, DC 20037, (202) 730-2500, isdc.com

BUTTERSCOTCH PUDDING

Serves 6

½ cup plus 3 tablespoons dark
    brown sugar, packed
3 tablespoons water
1¾ cups whole milk
½ cup heavy cream
¼ cup arrowroot
¼ teaspoon salt
3 egg yolks
3 tablespoons butter, unsalted,
    at room temperature and cut
    into 4 pieces
2 teaspoons vanilla extract
2 tablespoons light rum
Fresh whipped cream

Have six 3–4 ounce serving cups ready. (At RIS the pudding is served in martini glasses.) You will pour the pudding into them.

In a medium, heavy-bottom saucepan, put in the ½ cup brown sugar and water over medium heat and bring to boil. Stir to dissolve sugar, and boil for 2 minutes. Lower heat if necessary.

Add 1½ cups of the milk and all of the cream and bring to boil. Do not worry if the mixture curdles as it heats.

While milk is heating, put the arrowroot and salt into food processor and pulse. Pour mixture out of processor into small bowl, set aside.

Put the 3 tablespoons of brown sugar and yolks into the processor and blend for 1 minute. Scrape down sides of bowl with spatula, add remaining ¼ cup of milk and pulse to blend. Add the arrowroot and salt mixture to processor and pulse a few times.

With the machine running, very slowly pour in the hot mixture from the saucepan. Process for a few seconds and then pour everything back in saucepan.

Over medium heat, whisk constantly, making sure to get the edges of the pan, until pudding thickens and a few bubbles come up to the surface (about 2 minutes). You do not want the pudding to boil but you want it to thicken, so lower your heat if needed.

Scrape pudding back into processor. If you have a scorched spot in pan, avoid scraping it. Pulse a few times.

Add the butter, vanilla, and rum and pulse until all are evenly blended.

Pour pudding into cups. If you do not want skin to form on top, press a piece of plastic wrap against the surface of each pudding to create an airtight seal. Or you can cover the top of each cup with plastic wrap.

Refrigerate at least 4 hours before serving. (Covered pudding can be refrigerated up to 2 days.) Before serving, top each cup of pudding with fresh whipped cream.

CHICKEN POT PIE

Chef's note: "In my humble opinion, there should always be plenty of light, flaky crust in a chicken pot pie. Make plenty of your favorite pie dough or buy 100-percent butter puff pastry, rolled to ⅛ inch and cut to cover and/or encase individual ramekins or larger casseroles."

PIE DOUGH:

2 cups all-purpose flour (Ris uses King Arthur)
¾ tablespoon salt
⅓ pound pure lard
You can make your own pie dough or buy 100-percent butter puff pastry, rolled to ⅛-inch and cut to cover and/ or encase individual ramekins or larger casserole dishes.

FOR THE ROUX:

4 ounces butter
1 cup flour

Roll out the pastry to suit your needs and keep covered in the refrigerator until ready to use.

To prepare the roux: Melt the butter in a heavy-based saucepan over medium heat. Whisk in the flour, stirring constantly, spreading the paste over the bottom of the pan to lightly color and cook the flour, about 5 minutes. Set aside in a warm place until ready to use.

To prepare the filling: Roast the mushrooms and pearl onions in a 350°F oven until golden. Season with salt and pepper, fresh thyme, and olive oil. Set aside when done until ready to use.

In a heavy-based, 2-gallons soup pot or Dutch oven, melt the 2 tablespoons of butter and add the diced onions, celery, and carrots. Sprinkle with the chopped thyme and sage and cook until the onions are barely soft, stirring occasionally, just enough to release the aromatics from the vegetables, about 5 minutes. Add the chicken stock and bay leaf and bring to a boil. Let simmer for another 5 minutes to meld the flavors and season the stock.

Add the potatoes and any additional root vegetables. Season lightly with salt and fresh cracked pepper. Bring just to a boil and add the peas, roasted mushrooms, roasted pearl onions, and chicken meat. Bring back just to a boil again, keeping in mind that you have about 5 minutes to finish from the point of adding the potatoes before they are overcooked.

Thicken with the roux, whisking in a bit at a time and dissolving each bit, avoiding lumps. Taste for seasoning and adjust with salt, pepper, and a dash of sherry vinegar for brightness. Let cook a minute longer and remove from the heat.

To finish: Prepare your pastry to accommodate your vessel. Fill with the pot pie filling and cover with more pastry. Filling can be hot if put in the oven immediately or chilled and can be kept in the refrigerator until ready to use. Cooking time will be in a 350°F oven, but will depend on size of pie and whether or not filling was hot or cold. Individual portions take 20 minutes or so. Larger casseroles may take up to 1 hour or longer.

FOR THE FILLING (MAKES 3–4 QUARTS OR 6–8 SERVINGS):

8 ounces mushrooms, whole or quartered (if large)
1 cup pearl onions, peeled
Salt and freshly ground pepper
Fresh thyme
Olive oil
2 tablespoons butter
1 large onion, diced, about 2 cups
2 large stalks celery, cut in large dice, about 1 cup
2 carrots, cut in large dice, about 1 cup
2 tablespoons chopped fresh thyme
2 tablespoons chopped fresh sage
2 quarts chicken stock
1 bay leaf
1 large potato, cut in large dice, about 1 cup
1–2 cups, or to taste, root vegetables that are available: parsnip, celery root, sweet potato, or all of the above, peeled and cut in large dice
1 cup fresh or frozen English peas
2 cups roasted chicken meat, cut in large dice or shredded chunks
Sherry vinegar

Room 11

Something about the corner of 11th and Lamont Streets always called out to Ben Gilligan. Long before businesses started gravitating to that part of Northwest DC, the look and energy of the spot grabbed his attention. "I always liked the way it sat on the block, both unassuming and welcoming," he recalls. "It's not like I dreamed of opening a place there, I just thought it would be a good spot for something."

As what can either be described as foreshadowing or coincidence, or perhaps a touch of both, a storefront opened up on that fateful corner just as Gilligan, who had been working as an art handler, started getting the itch to come back to cooking after a ten-year hiatus. "I missed the pace of the kitchen," tells Gilligan, who worked as a cook in Australia where he spent much of his childhood. "It gets in your bones a little bit."

His background in construction and cooking made the Room 11 co-owner perfectly poised to open what turned out to be a little neighborhood wine bar with an everyone-knows-your-name vibe. "Someone once referred to it as a great, pinky-down wine bar," he shares.

Gilligan acted as general contractor for the project and along with his partners, staff, and friends did most everything, from laying the beautiful floors on up. The floors, a rustic work of art by themselves, Gilligan crafted from reclaimed yellow pine strips he found and cut into three-quarter-inch pieces to look almost like bricks. It's worth casting your eyes down when you walk in to soak up the handiwork and craft beneath your feet. He also helped put in the zinc bar. "I love old zinc," he says. "But it's like a brand new pair of Chuck Taylors at first. They are so clean it's embarrassing. But then they wear over with time."

A true jack-of-all-trades, Gilligan also was a member of the band French Toast, playing guitar, bass, and drums in addition to singing for the group that put out a couple of records on a local label. He also played guitar on the album Dust Galaxy, a side-project of Rob Garza's Thievery Corporation. "I have a philosophy degree so I have to do lots of different things," he jokes. "Not many jobs out there for philosophers."

3234 11th Street NW, Washington, DC 20010, (202) 332-3234, room11dc.com

MONSTER ISLAND COCKTAIL
Makes 1 Drink

This cocktail contains three strong flavors from famous islands and is garnished with a flamed orange peel. The Peat Monster whiskey is an homage to Godzilla and his island hometown of Tokyo.

1½ ounces Peat Monster scotch whiskey
1 ounce Averna Amaro Siciliano
2 dashes Angostura bitters
Orange peel

Combine first three ingredients in a mixing glass. Add ice, stir, and strain into a chilled cocktail glass. Garnish with a flamed orange peel.

CHARRED CAULIFLOWER SALAD WITH GARLIC CONFIT & TAHINI DRESSING

Serves 4–6

1 head garlic, plus 3 cloves for tahini dressing, peeled and left whole
1 bay leaf
1 sprig thyme
1 cup extra-virgin olive oil
2 lemons, zest and juice
½ cup tahini (sesame paste)
½ teaspoon smoked paprika
Salt and pepper
1 head cauliflower
½ cup vegetable stock or water
1 large bunch curly parsley

For the confit of garlic: Preheat oven to 225°F. Separate garlic head into cloves and peel the cloves. Place the peeled garlic into a small ovenproof saucepan with the bay leaf and thyme, cover with olive oil. Gently heat the saucepan until the garlic is just starting to show color. Place the saucepan on a low rack in the oven. Cook for 4 hours, or until the garlic is a nice warm brown. Remove from the oven and let cool completely. You can jar it now and it will keep for up to a month in the fridge.

For the tahini dressing: Combine the zest of 1 lemon and the juice of 1½ lemons (keep the other half for finishing), the 3 reserved garlic cloves, tahini paste, paprika, and a good pinch of salt and pepper in a food processor. Blend until smooth. Thin with up to ⅓ of a cup of warm water if the dressing seems too tacky. Taste for seasoning. It should be quite lemony and a little salty.

For the charred cauliflower: Turn the oven up to 475°F and heat a sheet pan on the top rack. Chop the cauliflower into bite-size florets or, for a more dramatic effect, cut them into large wedges as you would iceberg lettuce. Toss with just a little of the garlic confit oil. You want the cauliflower to char not fry, and avoid using the actual garlic cloves as they will burn. Spread cauliflower on the hot sheet pan and place in the oven for 8 minutes. Leave it alone. Let it stick to the pan. After a full 8 minutes, shake the pan to get everything moving. Cook for a further 7 minutes.

Remove pan from the oven and transfer the cauliflower to a large serving dish. Season with a little salt while it is still warm. Heat the sheet pan on the stovetop as you would when making gravy and add a couple big spoonfuls of the confit garlic cloves. Fry for 30 seconds before deglazing with the vegetable stock, making sure to scrape up all the yummy cooked-on bits. Pour the jus all over the cauliflower and spoon over the tahini dressing. Dust with paprika and finish with a ton of fresh parsley and the leftover half lemon, cut into wedges.

Even though this dish is vegan, somewhat by accident we've found it goes really well with grilled steaks.

Rosa Mexicano

Josefina Howard was ahead of the times. Back in 1984, when most people thought farm-to-table to be a string of words thrown together, the Rosa Mexicano founder insisted that the guacamole at her upscale Mexican restaurant be made tableside. Howard wanted her guests to see the caliber and freshness of the ingredients being used in what has become a signature dish for the restaurant that now claims many locations beyond that first one in New York City.

Creating a paste from the onions, cilantro, lime, and jalapeños stands as the first and really the key step in crafting the guacamole. "The proof is in the paste," says the restaurant's Executive Regional Chef Steven Lukis, who is one of the people charged with training staff in the art of making the popular avocado dip that comes served with house-made corn tortilla chips. "The paste is the secret to the guacamole."

Everyone who works at Rosa Mexicano must go through something of a guacamole boot camp, spending hour after hour, day after day, perfecting the technique needed to create the tableside dish. Special attention is paid to making the perfect paste and the technique of folding in the ingredients layer by later. Diners get to choose from three degrees of spice when they start their meal with the guacamole, and the staff learns to deliver the right amount of heat into each made-to-order batch. If you want to attempt the recipe at home, Lukis strongly recommends investing in a molcajete, a Mexican mortar and pestle carved from volcanic rock, an invention that dates back thousands of years and was used by both the Aztecs and Mayans.

575 7th Street NW, Washington, DC 20004, (202) 783-5522, rosamexicano.com

GUACAMOLE EN MOLCAJETE

Serves 4

FOR CHILI PASTE:

1 tablespoon finely chopped
  white onion
1 tablespoon chopped fresh
  cilantro
2 teaspoons finely chopped
  jalapeño, or more to taste
1 teaspoon salt, or as needed

3 medium-ripe but firm Hass
  avocados
3 tablespoons diced plum tomato
2 tablespoons chopped fresh
  cilantro
1 tablespoon finely chopped
  white onion
Salt if necessary

SPECIAL EQUIPMENT:
Molcajete

To prepare the chili paste: Grind the onion, cilantro, jalapeño, and salt together in a molcajete until all the ingredients are very finely ground. Alternatively, use a fork to mash all the ingredients to a paste in a wide hardwood bowl.

To assemble: Cut each avocado in half, working the knife blade around the pit. Twist the halves to separate them and flick out the pit with the tip of the knife. Fold a kitchen towel in quarters and hold it in the palm of your "non-knife" hand. Rest an avocado half, cut-side up, in your palm and make three or four evenly spaced lengthwise cuts through the avocado flesh, without cutting through the skin. Make four crosswise cuts in the same way. Scoop the diced avocado flesh into the molcajete. Repeat with the remaining avocado halves.

Gently fold the avocado into the paste, keeping the avocado in as large pieces as possible. Add the tomato, cilantro, and onion and fold in gently. Taste and add salt if necessary. Serve immediately, right from the molcajete or bowl, with chips and tortillas.

Soupergirl

What's the difference between a stand-up comedian and a vegetarian soup entrepreneur? I have no idea but chances are Sara Polon does. In fact, I bet the comic turned soup seller could nail that set up's punch line while at the same time whipping up a batch of gazpacho and stirring a steamy pot of mulligatawny stew. No word yet on whether she could do it while standing on one foot or with a hand tied behind her back, but my hunch is that she could. After all, they don't call her Soupergirl for nothing.

Washington-area native Polon made the unlikely leap from comic to soup cook following a four-year stint playing the New York City club circuit by night and working government contracts during day. Eventually, she tired of the grind and came back to DC to figure out what came next. A life-changing read of Michael Pollan's book *The Omnivore's Dilemma* provided the answer. Polon decided to join the local food movement and soon thereafter landed on the idea of starting an organic, vegan soup business that only used locally sourced and in-season ingredients. The only missing piece was pulling her mom, aka Marilyn Polon aka Soupermom aka the best soup-maker around, out of retirement. "So now she's allowed to say that I need a haircut or that she hates my shoes because I brought her out of retirement," Sara says.

The pair still cook together, mixing up soups for the subscription service and the shop where you can eat in or take out that week's soups. Marilyn came up with the secret to the West African Peanut Stew—lots of peanut butter and cutting the sweet potatoes into big pieces before cooking them together for a long, long time until they melt.

"It's really rich, people just go crazy for it," says Sara, adding that the first time they made the soup, which has turned into their best-seller, they were convinced it was going to bomb. "Now we always sell out. We have to brace staff when we put it on the menu."

Giving the audience what it wants, be it new material or West African Peanut Stew, is the similarity between stand-up comedian and a vegetarian soup entrepreneur. "At the end of the day the audience, or the customer, decides if you are a hit or a miss," she says. Thank you, Sara. We are glad that you and your soup will be here all week.

314 Carroll Street NW, Washington, DC 20012, (202) 609-7177, and 1829 M St NW, Washington, DC 20036, (202) 733-4401, thesoupergirl.com

WEST AFRICAN PEANUT STEW

Makes About 11 Cups

2 teaspoons canola oil

2 cups roughly chopped onion

1 tablespoon freshly ground cumin (toast the seeds and then grind them)

1 cup roasted peanuts, or ¾ to 1 cup of store-bought peanut butter (you can add more to taste)

6 cups peeled, cubed sweet potato (approximately 1-inch dice, large enough for the sweet potatoes to melt into the soup)

2 (15-ounce) cans chickpeas, drained

1 (28-ounce) can diced tomatoes

3½ cups vegetable broth (homemade please!)

½ teaspoon black pepper

¼ teaspoon salt

To begin the soup, heat oil in a stockpot over a medium-high heat. Sauté onions until very soft. Add the cumin and cook for another minute. Don't burn your spice!

Put peanuts in a blender and process to a paste. Add peanut butter, sweet potato, chickpeas, tomatoes, and broth to the pot. (If using commercial peanut butter, choose an all-natural brand—don't use Jif. Don't be afraid to use more as well—people love peanut butter!) Bring to a boil.

Reduce heat and simmer, uncovered, for 30 minutes, until the potatoes are soft—they should melt into the soup, which gives it a nice, natural sweetness.

Stir often to avoid burning! The soup is heavy and the ingredients can fall to the bottom of the pot and burn!

Season to taste—the seasoning listed above is just a guideline. If you make your own peanut butter, you might need a bit more salt.

Add more peanut butter if needed.

The Source by Wolfgang Puck

When Scott Drewno turned twenty-one, he left home, moved to Las Vegas, and fell in love. But Drewno's tale is not one of a quickie-wedding-chapel-Elvis-impersonator-what-happens-in-Vegas-stays-in-Vegas cliché. Instead Scott's story starts in the kitchen of Chinois, Wolfgang Puck's decidedly Elvis impersonator–free Asian fusion restaurant, where Scott worked as line cook, found a mentor, and discovered a whole new world of flavors he never knew about in the small upstate New York town where he grew up.

"I was taken aback and amazed by things like ginger and lemongrass and cooking with a wok and whole roasted duck," tells the soft-spoken executive chef of The Source, housed in the magnificent Newseum. "I fell in love."

Fast-forward some 20 years later and Drewno's love affair with Asian cuisine and techniques is still going strong. From his kitchen at The Source, the chef creates traditional Asian dishes with a modern, upscale flair. The chef's commitment to locally sourced ingredients also comes through in all of his dishes, including this one for Velvet Corn Soup.

Drewno based this recipe on a traditional velvet corn soup he tasted on one of his many trips to China. The luxurious mouthfeel of the dish won him over. The warm, creamy soup only appears on the menu during corn season, much to the dismay of its many fans. The good news is that other seasonally driven soups, like his spring pea, take its place when corn season comes to a close. For those who prefer a non-chicken stock, Drewno recommends creating a simple corn stock, as he often does. He recommends cooking corncobs, celery, onion, and carrots together, and then letting the stock simmer for an hour or two. Wearing your blue suede shoes as you stir also doesn't hurt.

Drew no longer is with The Source but his Velvet Corn Soup still is a crowd pleaser.

575 Pennsylvania Avenue NW, Washington, DC 20565, (202) 637-6100, wolfgangpuck.com/restaurants

VELVET CORN SOUP WITH
MARYLAND JUMBO LUMP CRAB & CHILI OIL

Makes 1½ Quarts

15 ears corn
1 small white onion
¼ pound butter
Sea salt and pepper, to taste
2 cups chicken stock
1 quart heavy cream
2 ounces per serving of
    Maryland jumbo lump
    crabmeat
Chili oil to taste
1 tablespoon chopped scallions

Grate corn on a box grater with large holes. Sweat out onions with butter over low heat. Add grated corn and sweat out. Season to taste with salt and pepper. Place stock and cream in a pot and bring to a boil, and then add hot cream and hot chicken stock to corn and onion mixture and simmer.

Adjust seasoning. Puree in blender and pass through a sieve.

Serve with crabmeat and garnish with chili oil and scallions.

Sticky Fingers Bakery

With cupcakes and kindness, Doron Petersan kills the notion that you can't make to-die-for baked goods without eggs and butter. Petersan, along with Sticky Fingers Bakery head baker Jenny Webb, beat out the conventional competition not once but twice for the win on the popular Food Network's Cupcake Wars, and awards dot the walls and website of the aqua and pink shop with its funky vintage diner–style vibe and neighborhood hangout feel. Even with all the titles and praise, it's the taste of the cookies, cakes, brownies, and other sweet treats sold at the vegan bakery that keep people coming back for more.

"If it didn't taste good, we wouldn't be here," says Petersan, the Sticky Fingers owner who is as delightful as the baked goods housed behind the counter of her Columbia Heights shop. File Petersan's bakery ownership under "necessity is the mother of invention." The native New Yorker started the dairy- and egg-free bakery in 2002 after taking the vegan plunge and not being able to find any yummy vegan desserts here in her new hometown of DC. She began the bakery in a small space on 18th Street with a business partner who left under good terms in 2009 to move to California to join an Iron Maiden tribute band. (File that under "happens all the time in the vegan bakery world.") "We started the place with a $20,000 loan, a very ambitious business plan, and a stupid amount of confidence," she laughs.

The unlikely approach paid off. In 2006, she opened the current spot and expanded the business to include savories and a sit-down area. Although she can whip up a sticky bun with the best of them, Petersan makes no bones, no pun intended, about her role.

"I'm not a pastry chef," she says. "I'm a business owner. I clean the bathroom and sign paychecks and run day-to-day errands. I go to Whole Foods and Home Depot. Most of what I do is say yes, no, good idea, or maybe try this."

Still, despite her downplaying her baking role, it's clear Petersan possesses quite a bit of her own kitchen wisdom. Before starting the business, the avid cyclist and mother of a young son studied food science and nutrition and worked as a baker and bartender. She attributes the leave-them-wanting-more taste of her baked goods to the techniques they use at the shop to create flavors rather than simply throwing in substitutions. "It's the way we incorporate the ingredients and mix them together that makes it work," she says.

Her love of simple yet delicious flavors like the ones she uses in this recipe she attributes to her family, and growing up in her family's strong Jewish and Italian (or Jewtalian, as she calls it) food culture.

1370 Park Road NW, Washington, DC 20010, 202-299-9700, stickyfingersbakery.com

BLOOMING CHERRY BLOSSOM CUPCAKES
(VANILLA CUPCAKE, TART CHERRY FILLING, ALMOND CRÈME FROSTING, AND TOASTED ALMONDS)

Makes 18 Cupcakes or two 9-inch round cakes

VANILLA CUPCAKE BATTER:
3 cups (11½ ounces) all-purpose flour
1 tablespoon baking powder
½ teaspoon salt
1⅓ cups sugar
½ (4 ounces) cup non-hydrogenated vegan margarine (Earth Balance brand recommended)
½ cup water
1½ teaspoons egg replacer (Ener-G brand recommended)
¾ cup soy milk
2 teaspoons vanilla extract

CHERRY FILLING
2 cups pitted cherries, fresh or frozen, pureed
1 tablespoon lemon juice
1 cup sugar
¼ cup water
¼ cup cornstarch

Preheat the oven to 350°F. Line two 9-inch round cake pans with parchment or place liners in cupcake trays.

Sift the flour, baking powder, and salt into a medium-size bowl. Set the bowl aside.

In the bowl of an electric stand mixer, cream the sugar and the margarine with the whisk attachment, about 5 minutes. Scrape down the sides and bottom of the bowl.

In a small bowl or cup, combine the water and egg replacer and stir to dissolve the egg replacer. Add the egg replacer to the sugar and mix until combined.

In a small bowl, combine the soy milk and vanilla and set aside.

Turn the mixer speed to low and slowly add the dry ingredients and the soy milk, alternating between the two, ending with the soy milk.

Fill lined cupcake tin ¾ full and bake for 16–19 minutes, or until toothpick inserted in the center comes out clean.

In a medium, heavy-bottom saucepot, stir together the cherries, lemon juice, and sugar. Heat on medium-high until the mixture begins to bubble around the edges.

In a small bowl, mix the water and cornstarch into a slurry.

Slowly add the cornstarch mixture to the cherries while whisking. Cook for 2 more minutes while stirring until it becomes pourable. Let cool completely. Makes about 2 cups.

In the bowl of a stand mixer, whip shortening and margarine with the paddle attachment until completely combined. Scrape the bottom of the bowl to ensure that all ingredients are mixed thoroughly.

On low speed, slowly add sugar a little at a time.

Once the sugar is incorporated, add the vanilla and almond extract and soy milk, one tablespoon at a time, and mix on low until the liquids are incorporated.

Scrape the bottom of the bowl and mix on medium-high speed until all ingredients are combined and frosting is fluffy, about 2 minutes.

Spread almonds on a baking sheet and bake for 10–15 minutes at 350°F. Let cool. Makes enough frosting to frost a 2-layer 9-inch cake or 18 cupcakes.

Assembly: Once cupcakes are cooled, using a paring knife or a frosting tip, poke a hole in the top center of the cupcake about ½ inch down into the middle. With a spoon or a pastry bag fill the hole with cherry filling, about 1 tablespoon. Frost your cupcake using a piping bag or spatula. Tip your cupcake and roll the frosting in the toasted almonds and coat as desired. Enjoy!

FROSTING

1 cup plus 2 tablespoons nonhydrogenated vegetable shortening (Earth Balance brand recommended)
¼ cup plus 2 tablespoons nonhydrogenated vegan margarine (Earth Balance brand recommended)
4½ cups 10x powdered sugar
3½ teaspoons vanilla extract
2 teaspoons almond extract
2 to 4 tablespoons soy milk, as needed
½ cup almond slices

Sunflower Bakery

Every morning it's back to school for Chef Elizabeth Hutter. The former Watergate Hotel pastry chef dons her apron and heads to the front of her industrial-kitchen-slash-classroom to teach the ins and outs of professional baking to her students, adults with development and other disabilities. But her lessons are not just a dry run. The Sunflower Bakery is a true working kitchen where the students fill customer orders each day with the delicious cookies, cakes, and other treats they bake as part of the nonprofit organization's on-the-job training program.

"We don't adapt the bakery to them," tells Hutter. "We plan our day based on the orders. The students are getting real job experience."

The experience proves to be invaluable. Sunflower graduates go on to get baking jobs at places like Safeway, Bundles of Cookies, and Stella's Bakery, where they put into action the skills they have learned from Hutter and the Sunflower team. "We train people to get out and work at other sites," she shares.

The Gaithersburg-based program runs a popular "sweets of the month" subscription program. You can either pick up your goodies at the bakery or at pre-designated drop-off locations around town. The program is particularly popular at, but by no means limited to, Jewish schools and synagogues as Sunflower is also a certified kosher bakery. As a result, all the items that come out of the kitchen are pareve, which means they contain no meat or dairy ingredients, including butter. The laws of keeping kosher dictate a strict separation between meat and any food containing milk products hence the need for neutral or pareve desserts that can be eaten in the same meal with either. Despite its kosher status, Sunflower is a nonsectarian organization and is open to students of all religions. Hutter, who herself is not Jewish, did a quick prep on substitutions and kosher laws before taking over the kitchen and adapts all the recipes they use to fit the standards as she did with this mandel bread. "Our mandel bread is really good, it's like a biscotti but not as hard," she says. "Margarine doesn't get as hard as butter so when you sub margarine in for butter, you wind up with a cookie that is going to be a bit more chewy. Ideally you should cut up your margarine like ice cubes and put it in the freezer for a half hour before using it. That way it's more like butter."

8507 Ziggy Lane, Gaithersburg, MD 20877, (240) 361-3698, sunflowerbakery.org

COMBO MANDEL BREAD

Makes About 8 Dozen Pieces

2¼ cups (12 ounces) all-purpose flour

1 cup (8 ounces) granulated sugar

1½ teaspoons baking powder

Pinch of salt

6 ounces cold salted margarine*

5 ounces dried cranberries

9 ounces semisweet chocolate chunks/chips

6 ounces slivered almonds (not sliced)

3 large eggs

1 teaspoon vanilla extract

*Margarine breaks down faster than butter, so you really have to keep the margarine cold. Put it in the freezer for half an hour before using and it will be more like butter.

Preheat the oven to 325°F. Line two half-sheet pans with parchment paper.

Combine the flour, sugar, baking powder, and salt in a 5-quart mixing bowl and mix well on low speed, using a paddle attachment. Cut cold margarine into small pieces and toss into the mixing bowl. Mix on low speed until the margarine is incorporated and the mixture is cool and powdery.

Pour in the fruit, chocolate, and nuts, mixing briefly to combine.

Whisk the eggs and vanilla together in a small bowl.

Beat in the eggs and vanilla to the margarine/flour mix on low speed, taking time to scrape the bottom of the bowl very well.

Turn the dough out onto a floured surface and knead it lightly, making sure that the fruit, nuts, and chocolate are evenly distributed. Divide the dough into four equal pieces, each weighing about 13 ounces. Roll each piece of dough into a smooth log about 12 inches long on a lightly floured board.

Place the logs on sheet pans lengthwise, spacing them 4 inches apart. Bake for 35–40 minutes or until the logs are golden and firm to the touch.

Remove pan from oven. Allow the logs to cool completely. (After they cool, they may be wrapped and frozen for finishing at a later date.)

Carefully place the cooled logs on a cutting board. Use a serrated knife to carefully cut the mandel into half-inch-thick slices. Arrange the cookies on the baking sheets, laying them flat.

Bake for a second time at 325°F until the mandel are golden, about 10–15 minutes. Cool the mandel completely before wrapping in airtight container.

Store cookies at room temperature for up to 5 days or freeze for up to 3 months.

Sweet Home Cafe

The museum experience does not end when you step into the cafeteria at the National Museum of African American History and Culture. A mural-sized photo of the Greensboro Four sitting in protest at a lunch counter graces the far wall and artifacts, historic photos, and memorabilia surround the rest of the 400-seat dining room. Food-related quotes among the objects and images share words of people like local food historian Michael W. Twitty, who pens the food blog Afroculinaria. "Our food is our flag. . . it sits at the intersection of the South, Africa, the Caribbean and Latin America," reads his quote. Taken together the words, objects, and images create the ideal backdrop for the heart of the cafe: an expertly curated menu that uses taste as a vehicle to teach.

"We view the cafe as an edible exhibit," says Sweet Home Cafe Executive Chef Jerome Grant.

Recipes prepared at the cafe illuminate parts of the African American experience. Together the dishes share a diverse collection of stories. The menu itself is divided into four regions. Items on the menu are associated with one of the four geographical areas—The Agricultural South, The Creole Coast, The North States, and The Western Range—and are the result of years of research guided by the scholarship of culinary historian Dr. Jessica B. Harris. For several years before the museum opened, Grant served on the team that helped curate the menu, which changes four times a year with the seasons.

"We are telling the story of the food, of comfort, and of history along with the story of why this table is so important," says Grant standing in the middle of the dining room of the cafe, which feeds about 2,000 visitors each day. "But we also elevate it to modern day."

The Agricultural South shines as the most popular menu section with the Buttermilk Fried Chicken holding the distinction of most ordered dish. Grants tells part of his own family's story in the "Smoking Hot Pepper Pot." "It is based on the oxtail pepper pot I grew up with," he says. "It resonates with me every day. It's the thing that still automatically stops me in my tracks. It brings me back to being a young boy running around my grandma's house."

Grant, who as a teenager worked as a short-order cook at the Andrews Air Force Base officers club, credits his grandma as the one who helped him understand flavors. An understanding that has helped him develop some of the other dishes at the cafe like the Pan Roast Rainbow Trout from the Western Range menu designed to illuminate what for some is lesser-known part of the African-American experience.

"After slavery was abolished, a lot of African-Americans migrated west for new opportunities," he tells. "The chuck wagon was under way. Cast iron cooking was really big. Many African-Americans cooked for the men working on the railroad... And, trout was rampant out there."

I'm concerned that Americans are losing that place of meeting. There are very few times we can be more intimate as to share food together.

MAYA ANGELOU

The **AGRICULTURAL SOUTH**

↑ Line Starts Here

Sweet Home Café

His Pan Roast Rainbow Trout recipe is a modern interpretation of the ingredients and cultural influences that existed at the time. The trout gets stuffed with day-old cornbread, mustard greens, and boiled and preserved tomatoes. It's topped with hazelnut butter. The corn pays homage to the Native American influence and some of the spices used are a nod to the Latin American and Asian American presence in the region.

"We took indigenous items available from that region and put them together in this dish," he explains.

While the food at Sweet Home Cafe comes from careful research, the chefs know the stories told through food are ones meant to evolve with the teller. "Our cooks are all into it. And it will continue to grow based on me, our sous chefs, and our cooks. This museum is special for a lot of us"

It's the individual connection that keeps the edible exhibit alive. Take Ms. Dionne's potato salad. It's the recipe belonging to a cafe staff member, Dionne Alleyne, one of the cooks in the kitchen who has long made the potato salad for her own family gatherings and touts a little pickle juice in the mayo (always Duke's) as part of its appeal. It's the same potato salad she serves to her family on special occasions although here she and the team make it for thousands a day.

Grant also feels connected to Sweet Home Cafe. "This is highly personal," he shares. "I set this as my goal. I am a kid from down the street in PG county. Now I get to tell the story of America."

National Museum of African American History and Culture, 1400 Constitution Ave NW, Washington, DC 20560, (202) 633-4751, nmaahc.si.edu/visit/sweet-home-cafe

PAN ROAST RAINBOW TROUT, CORNBREAD & MUSTARD GREEN STUFFING, HAZELNUT BROWN BUTTER

Serves 4

4 each rainbow trout 1 pound-
  size, butterflied
1 cup day-old cornbread
  croutons ⅛ inch sq
2 cups julienned mustard greens
½ cup yellow onions, julienne
½ cup tomato confit or sundried
  tomato
1 tablespoon olive oil
½ tablespoon sage, chopped
¼ cups hazelnuts, chopped
½ pound butter, cut into pieces
¼ cup sage, chopped
1 tablespoon lemon juice

For the Trout Stuffing: Cut the day old cornbread into small croutons and bake in the oven at a low temperature until thoroughly dried out, be sure not to allow them to get overly browned. Cool and reserve. In a skillet, cook the onions in the oil from the tomato confit until it becomes tender and caramelized, add the mustard greens and cook until wilted. Once the greens are done add the tomato, mix well and season. Remove from heat and allow to cool.

In a large mixing bowl add the onion, tomato and greens mixture, along with the chopped sage and cornbread croutons. Gently mix, being careful not to break up the mixture so that the stuffing can be identified with all the ingredients visible. Adjust seasoning as needed. Rest the stuffing for two hours prior to using to allow for the cornbread to absorb the liquid from the vegetables.

For the Trout: Place the trout dorsal fin down on the work table and open up the belly cavity. Confirm that it is free of bones and well trimmed. Season the fish then place approximately 3-ounces of stuffing into the fish cavity, spreading evenly across the filet. Fold over the other side of the fish on top of the stuffing and hand form to sculpt the look of a whole fish. Allow the fish to rest in the refrigerator with the stuffing for one hour prior to cooking.

Cooking the Trout: Preheat a sauté pan with some clarified butter. Once sufficiently hot, add the stuffed trout to the pan. Cook for approximately 3 minutes per side. The fish skin should be nicely browned and crisp. Transfer to a holding dish while the sauce is being made.

For the beurre noisette: In a hot pan, place the butter and allow to sizzle and turn brown. As it's just about all melted, add the hazelnuts and sage. Stir for a minute or two until butter is nice and brown. Add the lemon juice and stir for 30 seconds on high heat until incorporated. Drizzle mixture over the fish.

Tabard Inn

Memories at the Tabard Inn Restaurant are an off-menu item, but someone always seems to be ordering them up at the restaurant at the historic Dupont Circle hotel.

The staff reports hearing stories of people who dined or stayed at the eclectic forty-room inn, which is made up of three brick row houses. Recently a man who came in for dinner told a story of how he stayed at the Tabard Inn in 1974 when he was thirteen years old and how he vividly remembers gray and teal tiles on the floor. A little sleuth work in the office uncovered photos that unearthed a picture confirming his recollection.

The memories also extend behind the scenes of the restaurant. In the pastry section of the kitchen, a photo of a woman named Frances is affixed to the refrigerator door, watching over the busy chefs as they roll dough and plate desserts. Frances began her decades-long career at the Tabard Inn as a breakfast line cook in the late 1970s. Over the years she worked in several different departments until she retired not too long ago from accounts payable. Her picture, no doubt a caring tribute to a longtime colleague, stands as yet another literal and figurative snapshot of the Tabard Inn story.

Those coming in these days to make their own memories may want to opt for the coveted patio seating. The outdoor courtyard is dotted with art and found objects placed there by the Tabard Inn's on-staff curator, who has an eagle eye for the different and unusual. When it comes to art, menu, and memory at this N Street gem, you just never know exactly what you are going to find.

1739 N Street NW, Washington, DC 20036, (202) 785-1277, tabardinn.com/restaurant

POACHED EGGS WITH WILD MUSHROOM & ANCHO CHILI SALSA

Serves 8

FOR THE ANCHO CHILI SALSA:
3 tablespoons olive oil
½ cup wild mushrooms
1 shallot, diced
1 tablespoon epazote
Salt and pepper
2 ancho chilis
1 cup water
2 poblano chilis
4 plum tomatoes
4 cloves garlic
½ teaspoon salt
8 corn tortillas
8 eggs

FOR THE REFRIED BEANS:
2 cups dried black beans (you
    can also use pintos or
    another favorite bean)
6 cups chicken stock
1 tablespoon salt
1 yellow onion
1 jalapeño
4 garlic cloves
½ cup lard (or ¼ cup bacon fat
    and ¼ cup olive oil)
1 teaspoon ground cumin

To prepare the ancho chili salsa: Heat 3 tablespoons of olive oil in a pan. Sauté your favorite wild mushrooms for 2–3 minutes, along with shallot, epazote, and a pinch of salt and pepper.

Toast dried ancho chilis in the oven for 3 minutes at 300°F. Remove from the oven, remove the seeds, and then soak the chilis in ½ cup water. Once they are soft (this takes about 20 minutes), julienne the chilis and set them aside.

Rub poblano chilis with olive oil and roast them in the oven at 350°F, 10–15 minutes or until skins blister (or over a burner on the stove if you prefer). Cool the poblanos, peel them, and remove the seeds.

Roast plum tomatoes with cloves of garlic at 350°F for 20–30 minutes until the tomatoes are soft.

Place the roasted tomatoes and garlic and the ancho chilis in a blender or food processor with salt and ½ cup of water. Pulse only until coarsely chopped. Pour the mixture in a bowl and add the mushrooms and poblano chilis.

To prepare the refried beans: Soak the beans overnight. After the beans have been soaked, discard water. Take the soaked beans and simmer them in chicken stock and salt for about one hour until the beans are tender. Check that the beans are tender.

In a separate pan, roast 1 thickly sliced yellow onion, 1 jalapeño pepper, and peeled garlic. When the beans are tender, place them in a food processor with the onion, jalapeno, and garlic. Puree until smooth.

Refry the beans in lard (or a mixture of olive oil and bacon fat) and 1 teaspoon of ground cumin for 5–10 minutes, until it develops the consistency of thick paste.

Fry the corn tortillas in the same fat used for the beans until brown/crisp on both sides and poach the eggs.

To serve: Spread the refried beans on each tortilla and top with a poached egg and the chili salsa.

Housing WAVES

During World War II, the Tabard Inn served as a boardinghouse for seventy women from the Navy Women Accepted for Volunteer Emergency Service (WAVES), the nickname for an all-woman division of the US Navy formed during that war. The inn, first opened as a guesthouse in 1922, provided housing for these women serving their country for two years, from 1943 to 1945. WAVE Luella Moenter worked as a Cook 2nd Class in the Tabard Inn kitchen during those years and recently celebrated her ninety-fifth birthday with well wishes from the Tabard Inn staff.

STICKY TOFFEE PECAN PUDDING CAKE WITH NUTELLA GELATO

Makes Ten 8-Ounce Ramekins

12 ounces chopped dates
1½ cups boiling water
2 tablespoons vanilla extract
1½ teaspoons baking soda
6 ounces unsalted butter, room temperature
10 ounces granulated sugar
4 eggs, room temperature
2½ cups all-purpose flour
4 teaspoons baking powder
Pinch salt

FOR TOFFEE SAUCE:
12 ounces brown sugar
8 ounces butter, unsalted
6 ounces heavy cream
10 ounces toasted pecan pieces

SPECIAL EQUIPMENT:
Ice cream machine

NUTELLA GELATO
1¼ cups granulated sugar
1¼ cups water
1 vanilla bean, split
8 ounces Nutella

Preheat oven to 325°F. Combine dates, water, vanilla extract, and baking soda and let sit for 30 minutes.

Beat the butter and sugar in a mixer with paddle attachment until light and fluffy. Gradually (one at a time) add eggs and scrape bowl well.

Sift flour, baking powder, and salt. In two additions, add dates and flour. Scrape bowl and paddle well, until well incorporated

Coat 10 ramekins with nonstick cooking spray.

With a 3-ounce ice cream scoop, transfer batter to ramekins.

Bake 15–20 minutes or until middle bounces back when touched. Remove from oven and cool for 15 minutes.

To prepare toffee sauce: In a heavy-bottom pot, stir brown sugar, butter, and heavy cream over low heat until the sugar dissolves. Unmold cooled pudding cakes. Ladle ¼ cup of toffee sauce and a small handful of pecans into each ramekin. Place pudding cakes back into toffee-sauced ramekins.

Before serving, return to oven (325°F) for 5 minutes.

To serve: Invert ramekin to serving plate to release pudding cake.

To prepare the gelato: boil sugar, water and vanilla. Remove bean pod.

Let cool until cold.

Combine the Nutella and simple syrup in blender until smooth. Churn in an ice cream machine.

Taqueria Habanero

To listen to Mirna Montero's daughters talk about their mother is to hear the story of the American dream.

Montero worked for 18 years as a line cook at Jaleo, a job she started shortly after coming to this country from Mexico as a 20-year-old. At the downtown restaurant Alvarado met her husband, Dionicio "Dio" Montero, also a line cook who had immigrated to the United States from Mexico as a young adult. The couple married, had three daughters, and worked hard to give their family a good life.

"My mother knew she wanted to leave something for us," says Gabriela Montero, the middle child of the pair who, together, own and run Taqueria Habanero in Columbia Heights. "She wanted her daughters to go to university. She knew that would be hard to do working for another person."

So Mirna left Jaleo, which she refers to as "her school," to forge her own path among the DC food scene. The mother of three's hard work, skill, and motivation steered her successful journey from line cook to restaurant owner. Mirna sold food at construction sites and operated a food truck stocked with her tacos and tortas. She worked long hours with any eye toward perfecting her recipes and saving enough money to open her own place. In 2014 she signed a lease for a narrow space on 14th Street that housed a nail salon and Taqueria Habanero was born.

"When my mom was closing the restaurant the day of the grand opening she began to cry," recalls Yicela Montero, the couple's oldest daughter. "Her dream had come true. That day we all worked. My dad was the only cook and my mom was garnishing all the tacos. My sisters and I were taking orders, being the cashiers, and were working with the customers."

The simple hole-in-the-wall type spot serves the couple's version of Mexican street food. After opening its doors, Taqueria Habanero quickly earned the reputation of cooking up some of the best tacos in town and it's rare to see the eatery not packed. Some regulars drive in from Virginia for the tacos, tortas, huaraches, sopes, and quesadillas, the Monteros proudly tell. On a typical Saturday, more than 1,600 handmade tortillas are made on site and served to guests.

"It's what we always dreamed about," says Mirna. "Cooking our food and sharing it with people. As I look to the future I want to keep selling tacos and making the simple, humble food that we love."

All the food created in Taqueria Habanero's small open kitchen has been informed by the Monteros individual and shared experience both here and in Mexico. Dio, whose cooking style is more classical, sold tacos on the streets in Mexico when he was 14. Mirna takes a more modern approach to the genre but both share a commitment to serving an authentic cuisine. Although Mirna does admit there is something special they bring to each and every dish they make.

"Our secret is the time we put in and the ingredients we use," she shares. "But it's also the love and caring we add to everything."

It does not take more than a few minutes in the presence of this warm, strong, and talented woman to understand that this is true. Her cooking simply is independent confirmation.

23710 14th St NW, Washington, DC 20010, (202) 722-7700, Habanerodc

TACOS DE HONGOS

Serves 10–12

1 pound oyster mushrooms,
　julienned
1 pound shiitake mushrooms,
　julienned
1 pound white medium
　mushrooms, julienned
1 medium bunch of thyme –
　remove leaves from the stem
½ cup white onion, diced
8 diced garlic cloves
3 tablespoons of silver tequila
¼ cup of fresh lime juice
⅓–½ cup of olive oil for sautéing
Kosher salt to taste

TO FINISH:
20 corn tortillas
½ cup of minced cilantro
1 medium finely diced white
　onion
1 tablespoon of freshly made
　guacamole
Lime wedges and radishes for
　garnish

Wash and carefully dry all of the mushrooms before julienning. Heat large skillet or nonstick pan over medium-high heat and add olive oil. Once oil is hot, sauté the mushrooms, stirring occasionally for 6–8 minutes until light brown. Incorporate the diced onions. When the onions turns a light brown color, add the diced garlic. The onions can burn quickly if you are not careful so keep a close watch on the pan. After about two minutes, add the thyme leaves, tequila, lime juice. Add a dash of salt. Let the ingredients simmer until everything is golden brown. Turn off the heat. To assemble the tacos, spread guacamole on the tortillas first. Then spoon a layer of the mushroom mixture on top of the guacamole before folding. Garnish tacos with freshly chopped cilantro and onions.

Teaism

Linda Neuman, Michelle Brown, and Allison Swope met back in the days of shoulder pads at the Executive Club, a membership club for local professional women. Michelle managed the restaurant, Alison was the chef, and Linda worked in the restaurant at the Dupont Circle club, which had a workout room and a restaurant. It was the summer of 1984. "That was when the restaurant industry seduced me away from my degree in economics," says Linda, who was a Georgetown student at the time.

Later on, the three women worked together at Michelle's restaurant New Heights, and now, more than 25 years later, the trio is happily reunited at Teaism, the teahouse Michelle and Linda opened in 1996. The three women run the charming teahouse, examining everything that comes into the kitchen to make sure it is whole, organic, and unprocessed. "Allison and Michelle are so rigorous about scrutinizing our ingredients, making sure nothing has trans fats, high fructose corn syrups, additives, or is genetically modified," Neuman says.

The countries where tea comes from serve as the inspiration for the menu. "People tend to think Britain when they think tea, but tea doesn't grow in England," Neuman points outs. "It grows in places like China, Vietnam, Japan, and India."

The Teaism team approaches its tea offerings much like a wine list, refining and tasting the selections all the time for color, clarity, and brew. "Tea, like wine, is an agricultural product," she explains.

2009 R Street NW, Washington, DC 20009, teaism.com

BUCKWHEAT & HEMP HEART PANCAKES

Makes Approximately ten 5-Inch Pancakes

FOR APPLE COMPOTE:
6 Granny Smith apples, peeled,
    cored, cut into 8 wedges
    each
½ cup brown sugar
1 teaspoon cinnamon

FOR PANCAKES:
1½ cups buckwheat flour
1½ cups pastry flour
1 tablespoon baking powder
1 teaspoon baking soda
½ teaspoon salt
2 cups buttermilk
4 eggs
1½ cups milk
2 tablespoons honey
¼ cup rice bran oil
1 cup hemp seeds
Dried cranberries
Maple syrup

To prepare the compote: Place all ingredients in small sauté pan over medium heat.

Stir occasionally as the apples begin to release their juices. Simmer for approximately 10 minutes. Apples should be cooked, but not mushy.

To prepare the pancakes: Mix flours, baking powder, baking soda, and salt in bowl. In a separate bowl, beat together the buttermilk, eggs, milk, honey, and oil. Stir the wet ingredients into the dry ingredients, only enough to blend, do not overmix. Gently stir in the hemp seeds. Cook batter in desired-size pancakes on a hot griddle or in a hot pan.

Serve with warm apple compote, dried cranberries, and real maple syrup.

Sew Your Salty Oats

The Salty Oat Cookies sold at Teaism are the kind of cookies legends are made of. Online, loyal fans of the thick, chewy, raisin-filled cookie hypothesize about the well-guarded recipe and many a post has been devoted to broadcasting praises of the iconic treat.

Terri Horn, a former Washingtonian who worked as a pastry chef at places like Marvelous Market and 1789, is the mastermind behind the cookie. She developed the recipe over several years and when Teaism opened, she allowed the store to sell the salt-dotted creations. The shop, which keeps a backup ingredients list in case the items on the Horn-approved list are not in stock, jumped at the chance. Teaism pays Horn, who now lives in Maine and owns Kayak Cookie, a royalty for each and every salty oat cookie sold. Four times a year Horn goes down to DC to do quality-control checks and make sure the cookie is holding true to her well-guarded recipe. "We sold 158,000 last year or about 13,000 a month," says Neuman. With those kinds of sales, it's no wonder the Teaism team is contractually obligated to keep the recipe a secret.

Ted's Bulletin

If sprinkles on Pop Tarts and meat loaf with ketchup get you humming about a few of your favorite things, then you should get your gravy-loving soul to Ted's Bulletin as soon as possible. The Barrack's Row diner-style restaurant offers a menu of old-school American dishes against the backdrop of a 1930s-style decor. The Shake-N-Bake Fried Chicken stands out as a favorite among this menu of favorites. Added bonus: It even comes wrapped in paper minus the string.

"I definitely grew up eating Shake 'n Bake and I loved that herby flavor it would always have," says Chef Eric Brannon who came up with this retro dish served at Ted's Bulletin, a twist on the old suppertime standby. "When we came up with our menu we thought about the things we loved eating growing up...this was one of them."

Brannon's recipe also contains a pickle brine shout out to a fast food chicken he liked. When he discovered that back in the day the readymade chicken he enjoyed was pickle-brined before it was fried, he decided to do the same with the fried chicken he created for Ted's. The brining adds a hint of flavor and also helps tenderize the meat. For those attempting the recipe at home, he encourages using a whole chicken, assuring first-timers that cleaning a whole chicken really is a lot easier than people think. (It's also a lot cheaper than buying the pieces already cut and cleaned.) If you are feeling adventurous and want to give it a try, Brannon suggests doing a search online for video that walks you through the steps—there are many out there although none that I can find at this time done to Julie Andrews's tunes.

505 8th Street SE, Washington, DC 20003, (202) 544-8337, tedsbulletin.com

SHAKE-N-BAKE FRIED CHICKEN

2 Fried Breasts, Wings, Legs, and Thighs

1 whole chicken, quartered
1½ cups seasoned flour (see recipe below)
1 cup egg wash (see recipe below)
Brine (see recipe below)
1½ quarts vegetable oil for frying

FOR SEASONED FLOUR:
½ cup cornmeal
½ cup Italian seasoned bread crumbs
2 cups all-purpose flour
1 tablespoon Cajun spice
2 teaspoons chopped rosemary
2 teaspoons chopped thyme
2 teaspoons chopped parsley
1 teaspoon dried oregano
1 tablespoon salt
1 teaspoon black pepper

FOR THE EGG WASH:
5 eggs
3 ounces water
2 tablespoons hot sauce

FOR THE BRINE:
2 cups pickle juice
4 cups water
3 sprigs rosemary
2 sprigs thyme
1 tablespoon salt
1 tablespoon pepper

To prepare the seasoned flour: Mix all ingredients together until well incorporated.

To prepare the egg wash: Mix all ingredients together until well incorporated.

To prepare the brine: Mix all ingredients together until well incorporated.

To assemble: Cut chicken, place in brine, and refrigerate for 2 hours. Heat fryer or oil in a deep frying pan to 275°F.

Dredge chicken in seasoned flour, then in egg wash, then back in the seasoned flour until well coated. Place chicken in oil and fry for 12–14 minutes until golden brown and cooked all the way through. Use caution when frying and keep water away from oil. Only use a pan that has enough depth to leave half of the pan without oil.

After frying is complete, keep chicken warm in oven or let rest for 4 minutes before serving. Enjoy with your favorite dipping sauces.

Thip Khao

There are an unthinkable number of steps between a refugee camp and the pages of Bon Appétit magazine. Chef Seng Luangrath has walked them all.

In 1981, when she was just 12 years old, Luangrath and her family fled their home in the middle of the night. As was the case for so many others in Lao at the time, life had become unbearable when the Communist Pathet Lao regime took over the country that had already been ravaged by the Vietnam War and a bloody civil war. After escaping, Luangrath and her family found themselves in two different refugee camps in Thailand before immigrating to the United States. There, a young Luangrath living among other Laotians forced from home, found what became her lifelong art and passion: cooking the food of her homeland for others.

"In the first camp we had no supplies and food was passed out," says Luangrath. "We ate rice and soup. But in the second camp, we got supplies. An aid organization gave out uncooked food, some vegetables, pots, and pans."

The small freedom to cook her own meals, coupled with the kitchen skills she learned in Lao from her grandmother, opened up Luangrath's world in the most unlikely of places. "It was from watching my neighbors in the camp cook that I learned," tells Luangrath. "From each family I learned a different part of the Laotian cooking tradition. I was from the city and had never been to the country before. The people in the refugee camps were from all parts of Lao."

Luangrath and her family spent two years in the camps before the United States granted them asylum. The family moved to the San Francisco area where she continued to be in charge of meals. "My mom worked two jobs so my responsibility was to go to school, come home, do homework, and then prepare and cook for my whole family."

It doesn't seem like a stretch to say that many in Luangrath's situation would be weighed down by the responsibility or grow to resent being in a kitchen at all. But for the woman who is credited with launching the Lao food movement in this country, the opposite happened. "When I cook it feels like happiness to me," Luangrath says with a smile.

Several years after settling in the United States, Luangrath met her husband through an arranged marriage. The couple moved to the DC area where she once again embraced the role of caretaking through food preparations, orchestrating traditional Laotian feasts for her extended family during weekend gatherings. She loved to research and recreate dishes, teaching herself various techniques and tinkering with flavor combinations. Along the way, she had several jobs, including working at a bank and at a flooring business with her husband but all the while dreamed of owning her own restaurant. A dream that she says she has had for almost as long as she can remember. So much so that it spilled out into other places in her life. Luangrath often would cook or cater for clients and would routinely hear a chorus of people telling her she was in the wrong line of work.

The couple threw around the idea of Luangrath opening her own place, but the timing and financing never lined up in the right way. In 2009 they agreed that she would take some time off to see if she could translate dream into reality. "I did a lot of research on Laotian food. I read and practiced and tested recipes in my small kitchen."

Then the call came and a quick decision needed to be made. The Luangrath's goddaughter phoned with the news that Bangkok Golden, a Thai restaurant in Falls Church, was available. The chef knew that a Thai kitchen setup would make it easy for her to prep Laotian cuisine and the amount of money needed equaled the amount of money she had in the bank.

"Less than an hour later we had cut a deal," she recalls. "I thought I have to listen to my gut instinct and do it."

At first, Luangrath continued operating Bangkok Golden as a Thai restaurant while fashioning a "secret" Laotian menu for those in the know. The chef introduced new dishes slowly, adding a few at a time to measure if an audience existed for it. Before long the "off menu" become Falls Church's worst kept secret. Word of mouth and social media made stars of Bangkok Golden's Laotian dishes and the woman responsible for them.

The Thip Khao chef exudes a gentle mix of warmth and passion for her craft and her customers. And, one moment in the chef's kitchen reveals the depth that she brings to the dishes she creates.

Once the restaurant gained popularity, many of the DC regulars began asking for a location closer to home. A loyal customer helped make it happen. "A couple from DC said 'we will help you find a place,'" she tells. "They brought in a map and gave me details about DC neighborhoods. We got to DC with the full support of our guests."

In 2014 Luangrath opened Thip Khao, a Laotian restaurant, in Columbia Heights. Named for the traditional baskets used to hold sticky rice, Thip Khao was an immediate success with customers and critics. The restaurant even got nominated as one of Bon Appétit's best new restaurants, an honor Luangrath first thought was someone putting her on.

"I ignored it," Luangrath says of the emails she received from a reporter about the honor. "I thought it was a joke. I had no idea Bon Appétit was there. When the news came out I was in bed and I almost fell out of bed. I didn't believe it. I thought this is a dream. It is beyond, beyond, beyond, my hopes and dreams to get nationwide attention in Bon Appétit magazine."

Following the article, reservations got harder to secure and the chef's son, also a chef, Bobby Pradachith, joined the team. Everyone from Supreme Court justices to neighborhood regulars continue to frequent Thip Khao and its creator has been credited with bringing Lao food to table, pun very much intended. But the soul and intent of the place remains the same even as the scope has broadened.

The Thip Khao chef now travels back to her homeland to research and recharge as well as volunteer. There, she is involved with a food education program and the building of a new school. The Thip Khao chef's biggest joy still seems to come from being in the kitchen at her DC restaurant, and on days when it's closed, at Bangkok Golden. For Seng, it's the best way she knows to share her deep-rooted love of her homeland and food.

"I want people to experience our culture through our food," says Seng who also is a James Beard nominee. "When people ask me where I am from when I say Lao I have to explain where Lao is."

Thip Khao and Seng are helping to change that one dish at a time.

3462 14th Street, NW, Washington, DC 20010, thipkhao.com

KHAO SOI

Serves 5

PORK SOUP

4 quarts water
1½ pounds pork shank bones
1 each white onion, cut in ¼
1 stalk lemongrass, cut to 1-inch
    in length
4 ounces cilantro (stems and
    leaves)
½ cup fish sauce
Salt, to taste

SAUCE

4 tablespoons vegetable oil
3 tablespoons Korean red pepper
    fine powder (or paprika)
5 cloves of garlic, chopped
2 medium-sized shallots,
    chopped
1 cup pork, minced
1 cup fermented bean paste
1 cup tomato paste
1 tablespoon sugar

Rinse the pork bones under cold water and place in a medium-sized stock pot with 4 quarts of cold water. Bring up to a boil and reduce heat to a simmer. Simmer for three hours. Occasionally, remove any form of impurities on the surface of the broth.

After three hours, add the white onion, lemongrass and cilantro. Continue to simmer for one hour.

To finish, season the broth with fish sauce and enough salt to your preference.

Use immediately. If not, cool the broth down to room temperature and store in the refrigerator. The broth can last for up to a week. To store for longer periods of time, equally disperse the broth to large Ziplock bags and store in the freezer.

In a medium-sized sauce pan, bring the oil to a high heat. Add the shallots to caramelize to a golden brown color. Then add the garlic and cook until aroma is present. Add the fermented bean paste and tomato paste. Saute both with the shallots and garlic. Reduce the heat to medium and add the pork to let it slowly braise in the sauce. Once the pork is fully cooked, add the final seasoning of the Korean chili powder and sugar.

Use immediately. If not, cool the sauce to room temperature and store in the refrigerator for up to 3 months.

To assemble: Heat a large pot of water to a boil and cook the noodles for about 5–7 seconds. Bring the pork soup and sauce to a medium simmer. Taste to adjust seasoning. Place the noodles first in the bowls and pour the soup on top. Finish with a spoonful of the sauce (about 4 ounces). Finish off by topping the noodle soup with the garnishes. Serve immediately.

WIDE RICE NOODLES
5 12-oz portions

Note: You can find wide rice noodles at your local Asian supermarket. It is better to use fresh rice noodles (usually are packed and compressed). If not found, any rice-based noodles are acceptable.

GARNISHES
2 pints Hon Shimeji mushrooms
(or any mushroom)
8 ounces cilantro, chopped
4 ounces green onions, rough chopped
4 ounces fried garlic
4 ounces puffed rice

Vidalia

It seems only natural that a restaurant named for a variety of onion would feature said onion on its menu. But shining a spotlight on the restaurant's namesake was not part of the original plan at Vidalia.

"The baked Vidalia onion was Sallie's idea," tells Chef Jeffrey Buben, who co-owns the Southern-focused restaurant with his wife, Sallie. "We at the restaurant balked at it at first, thinking who is going to come in looking for a baked onion? The first night at Vidalia everyone asked where the baked onion was on the menu. The very next day we formulated the prototype for Vidalia's baked onion and it's been a staple ever since."

Rather than just rest on the success of that first onion dish, Buben made the decision to add a new one every year. "We did not want to be complacent so we have a contest each year for the staff to come with new variations of the baked onion."

Vidalia's Baked Onion with Spring Garlic Shoots, Mushrooms & Red-Eye Gravy is a recent winner and combines many of the tastes that have kept Vidalia a DC favorite since it first opened its doors back in 1993. When you make the winning recipe at home, remember to let the onions sit in their own liquid after removing them from the oven, which allows them to retain their juices and flavors. The onion-savvy chefs at Vidalia also advise leaving a bit of the root intact so that the onion stays together. It also makes for a prettier final presentation.

After more than two decades, Vidalia closed its doors in 2016.

1990 M Street NW, Washington, DC 20036, (202) 659-1990, vidaliadc.com

BAKED ONION WITH SPRING GARLIC SHOOTS, MUSHROOMS & RED-EYE GRAVY

Serves 8

4 jumbo Vidalia onions
¼ cup extra-virgin olive oil
2 cups king trumpet or shiitake mushrooms, washed and sliced
1 cup spring garlic shoots (or leeks), washed and chopped
2 slices country ham, julienned
¼ cup sherry vinegar
1½ cups beef broth or bouillon
½ cup strong black coffee
¼ cup light brown sugar
½ cup tomato, peeled, seeded and chopped
2 teaspoons fresh thyme, chopped
2 teaspoons fresh rosemary, chopped
Salt and freshly ground pepper to taste
4 teaspoons chives, minced

Preheat oven to 375°F. Peel the onions and remove core. Trim the bottom of the onion as close to the base of the onion as possible without causing the petals to separate. This will allow it to lay flat, but stay intact.

Heat the extra-virgin olive oil in a large saucepan or oven roaster pan over medium-high heat and place the onions in the pan, core side down. Add the mushrooms, spring garlic shoots, and country ham. Stir until they begin to brown slightly—this should take about 2–3 minutes. Add the vinegar, beef broth, coffee, and brown sugar. Stir into mixture until the sugar dissolves. Add the tomato, thyme, and rosemary. Season mixture with salt and pepper to taste. Cover the pan with aluminum foil.

Place the covered pan in the oven. Baste the onions with the pan liquid periodically until they are tender—about 45 minutes to 1 hour.

Remove the pan from the oven and let rest for 10 minutes. Transfer the onions to a serving plate. Place the pan with liquid back on medium-high heat and reduce slightly until a light glaze occurs, about 2–3 minutes. Adjust seasoning to taste and spoon the mixture over the onions.

Sprinkle with minced chives and serve.

Volt

The popular reality show Top Chef put Bryan Voltaggio's face on TV, but it was his ability to take farm-to-table dining off script that placed him at the top of the restaurant scene before the cameras ever switched on. After climbing the ranks of prestigious Manhattan kitchens, Bryan moved back to his hometown of Frederick, Maryland, to open Volt in 2008. The phone lines have been buzzing ever since.

One of those early calls came from the Top Chef producers, inviting him to compete on the show after realizing they had hit reality show gold: brothers who are both chefs. "They basically called me up and asked me do you want to come on the show and kick your brother's ass," he says with a slight smirk as he bends down and picks fallen leaves out from the raised beds in the garden beside Volt. In the end, Bryan came in second to his brother, Chef Michael Voltaggio, but he is quick to say he looks back at it as a fun and worthwhile experience. That was back in 2009 and diners and critics still can't get enough of the restaurant from the chef with inked-up arms and laser-beam focus. Volt still ranks as an "it" reservation for Washingtonians despite the forty-five-minute drive up north to get there, and a coveted spot at Table 21, the Chef's Table, still is considered serious foodie street cred.

Although his other ventures and commitments take him away from Volt, his staff knows the kitchen is the prize on days he is in the house. Come three in the afternoon on most days when he's at Volt, Voltaggio and his intense focus are in the kitchen of the restaurant he opened in the town where he grew up. Turns out you can go home again.

228 North Market Street, Frederick, Maryland 21701, (301) 696-8658, voltrestaurant.com

CRAB SUMMER ROLL

Serves 4

FOR CRABMEAT:
1 teaspoon grape-seed oil
½ shallot, minced
1 cup crabmeat
1 tablespoon spicy aioli (recipe below)
⅛ teaspoon salt
1 cilantro sprig, picked leaves only

FOR YUZU VINAIGRETTE:
3 ounces yuzu juice
3½ ounces orange juice
1½ ounces fresh ginger, peeled and chopped
2 stalks lemongrass, chopped
1 teaspoon sugar
¼ bunch cilantro
¼ teaspoon Dijon mustard
2 cups blended vegetable oil

FOR AIOLI:
3 whole large eggs
4 large egg yolks
2 tablespoons chili powder
½ teaspoon sriracha
1 tablespoon mae ploy
1 tablespoon plus 2 teaspoons salt
1¾ cup grape-seed oil

To prepare the crabmeat: Put the grape-seed oil in a small sauté pan set over medium heat. Once the oil begins to shimmer, add the shallot and cook 3–5 minutes until tender but not browned. Let the shallot cool to room temperature. Put the crabmeat in a mixing bowl, gently picking through it to remove any stray bits of shell or cartilage. Add the shallots, aioli, salt, and cilantro. Gently mix everything together. Store in a lidded container in the refrigerator for up to 2 days.

To prepare the yuzu vinaigrette: Put the yuzu juice, orange juice, ginger, lemongrass, and sugar into a saucepot set over medium heat and bring to a simmer. Cook until the liquid is reduced by half—about 10 minutes. Remove from the heat, add the cilantro and let cool to room temperature—about 20 minutes. Strain the liquid and transfer it to a small mixing bowl. Add the Dijon mustard and whisk them together. Once fully incorporated, slowly whisk in the oil until it has all been emulsified into the mustard mixture. Reserve.

To prepare the aioli: In a blender combine the 3 whole eggs, egg yolks, chili powder, sriracha, mae ploy, and salt. Turn the blender on low speed and slowly increase to a medium speed. Drizzle in the oil in a slow, steady stream until emulsified. Use immediately or transfer to a lidded container and store in the refrigerator for up to three days.

To prepare the soy air: Put the water, soy sauce, soy lecithin, and mirin in a tall, narrow container. Blend with an immersion blender to form a light, airy foam.

To make the avocado wrap: Peel avocados but leave them whole. Using a peeler, peel the avocado flesh in long thin strips. Line on a piece of square parchment that has been seasoned with oil to help release.

To finish: Lay one sheet of rice paper that has been soaked and is ready to be worked on a cutting board. On one side, lay ¼ inch of mixed crab on top and shape it to cover the width of the paper at 3½ inches. Roll the paper with crab inside to resemble a sushi roll. Cut into three even pieces. Place the avocado strips on the plate in a snake-like shape. Place the three pieces of crab roll around the avocado, one on each end and one near the middle of the avocado. Pour yuzu vinaigrette into a squeeze bottle to put six dots on the plate around the components. Garnish with micro cilantro, buzz the soy air with an immersion blender to refresh. Scoop foam off the top with a spoon and place two large spoonfuls on top of the two crab rolls.

FOR SOY AIR:
10 tablespoons plus 1 teaspoon water
5 tablespoons soy sauce
½ teaspoon soy lecithin
1 tablespoon mirin

FOR AVOCADO WRAP:
3 avocados
1 teaspoon grape-seed oil
Rice paper
Micro cilantro

Whisked!

Jenna Huntsberger did the baker's equivalent of running away and joining the circus. After coming to DC from Oregon to work for political advocacy groups, the pull of butter artfully mixed with sugar got the best of her and she left the world of 9-to-5 (it's DC so make that 9-to-9) for the world of oven timers and parchment paper. Huntsberger left the allure of political organizations to break into the world of food. She started her Modern Domestic blog and took on a series of part-time jobs that required her to spend her days in or near kitchens. Among them were stints at SouperGirl and The Big Cheese food truck before going out on her own to start her pie-focused business, Whisked!.

Her time at Soupergirl and The Big Cheese each helped carve out the path that led to Whisked! Like Soupergirl, Huntsberger operates on a subscription basis where customers pre-order pies—savory and sweet—and then pick them up at predetermined locations. (She also sells her baked goods at the Bloomingdale Farmers' Market.) The service recently morphed into the area's first pie CSA. Huntsberger scours the markets for the freshest ingredients of the moment, bakes them into her perfectly constructed pie crusts, and then offers them to her subscribers. It's her way of baking what is best and local into her business.

While Soupergirl serves as something of the business model and mentor, it's The Big Cheese that sparked the idea for the Nutella Banana Pie, her most popular dessert. The truck offered a Nutella banana desert sandwich, and while she was making them in the mobile kitchen one day it occurred to her that the combination would also make a great pie filling.

"I made it a bazillion times," she recalls. "So I asked my boss if I could steal his flavor combo and make it into a pie."

14th & U St NW, Washington, DC 20009, (202) 656-4890, whiskeddc.com, @whiskeddc

BROWNIE SANDWICH COOKIES

Makes 26 Halves, 13 Cookies

COOKIES:

2 cups all-purpose flour

½ cup (1½ ounces) cocoa
    powder, sifted

2 teaspoons baking powder

½ teaspoon salt

16 ounces semisweet chocolate
    chips, melted

4 eggs

2 teaspoons vanilla extract

2 teaspoons espresso powder

10 tablespoons (5 ounces) butter,
    softened

½ cup (3½ ounces) granulated
    sugar

1¼ cups (10½ ounces) dark
    brown sugar

VANILLA CREAM:

8 ounces (2 sticks) butter,
    softened

3 cups (12 ounces) powdered
    sugar

1 teaspoon vanilla extract

¼ teaspoon kosher salt

SPECIAL EQUIPMENT:

A number 20 scoop

To prepare the cookies: Preheat the oven to 350°F. In a medium bowl, whisk together the all-purpose flour, cocoa (sift the cocoa if it is lumpy), baking powder, and salt.

Place semisweet chocolate chips in a small bowl and microwave on low power, for 20 seconds. Remove from microwave and stir, then microwave for another 20 seconds on low power. Repeat melting and stirring process until chocolate is completely melted.

In a small bowl, gently mix the eggs and vanilla extract. Sprinkle over the espresso powder to dissolve.

In the bowl of a stand mixer fitted with a paddle attachment, cream the butter, sugar, and dark brown sugar until fluffy. Add the egg mixture and beat until combined, scraping down the sides of the bowl if needed. Beat in the melted chocolate until combined.

Gradually add the flour mixture until combined.

Let batter sit for half an hour to set before scooping with a number 20 cookie scoop. Place halves on a baking sheet lined with parchment paper, leaving at least 2 inches between cookies. Bake for 16–18 minutes, until edges are set but centers still look slightly raw. Let cool completely before filling with vanilla cream.

To prepare the vanilla cream: In the bowl of a stand-up mixer fitted with a paddle attachment, beat the butter until creamy. Add the powdered sugar and beat until light and fluffy, about 5 minutes. Beat in vanilla extract and kosher salt until combined.

NUTELLA BANANA PIE

Makes one 9-Inch Pie

FOR THE CRUST:
½ cup plus 2 tablespoons
   (3 ounces) graham cracker
   crumbs
1 tablespoon plus 1½ teaspoons
   (¾ ounce) dark brown sugar
Pinch of salt
2½ tablespoons (1¼ ounces)
   butter, melted

FOR THE NUTELLA LAYER:
1 ounce semisweet chocolate
4 ounces Nutella

To prepare the crust: Preheat the oven to 350°F. In a large bowl, mix together the graham cracker crumbs, dark brown sugar, and salt until evenly combined. Pour in the melted butter and mix into the dry mixture—crumbs should be damp and clump together if you pinch them with your fingers.

Carefully pat the crust mixture into the sides and bottom of a pie tin.

Bake for 10 minutes, until the crust is lightly toasted. Let cool.

To prepare the Nutella layer: In a small bowl microwave the chocolate on a low-power setting in 10 second intervals until melted, stirring occasionally. Stir into the Nutella until combined. Reserve 2 tablespoons of the mixture for garnishing the tart and carefully spread the remaining Nutella mixture in an even layer on the bottom of the crust (the easiest way to do this is to gently spread the filling with lightly wet fingers).

To prepare the banana pudding: Place the bananas in a shallow baking pan and sprinkle with the 1 tablespoon of sugar. Roast for 20–25 minutes until bananas are soft and sugar is caramelized. Transfer to a food processor and process until smooth.

In a saucepan, combine the ⅓ cup plus 1½ teaspoons of sugar, cornstarch, and salt. Whisk in the yolks. Gradually pour in the whole milk and evaporated milk, whisking until combined.

Heat mixture over moderate heat and bring to a simmer. Stir continuously as the mixture thickens. Let simmer for 1 minute, until the mixture is shiny and the cornstarch is cooked through. Take off the heat and mix in butter and vanilla extract.

Pour the mixture into the food processor and process with the banana until smooth. Strain and pour into the graham cracker crust, over the Nutella layer. Smooth top with a small offset spatula. Place plastic wrap directly on the surface of the pudding topping and refrigerate until set, about 2 hours.

To assemble: When set, drizzle or pipe the remaining Nutella mixture over the top of pie decoratively and garnish with chopped hazelnuts. Serve chilled.

FOR THE BANANA PUDDING:
1 large, very ripe banana (4 ounces), sliced lengthwise
1 tablespoon sugar (for sprinkling on bananas)
⅓ cup plus 1½ teaspoons (2½ ounces) sugar (for the pudding)
2 tablespoons (½ ounce) cornstarch
⅛ teaspoon salt
2 egg yolks
1 cup whole milk
¼ cup evaporated milk
2 tablespoons (1 ounce) butter
½ teaspoon vanilla extract

FOR THE GARNISH:
¼ cup hazelnuts, lightly toasted and roughly chopped

Zaytinya

At first glance it could have been a scene playing out in almost any living room in almost any town, anywhere in America. A then nine-year-old Michael Costa was glued to his family's TV, completely absorbed in the program before him. But when you zoomed in on the action, it wasn't a sitcom or a tied game that was drawing him in. Instead it was a chef preparing a chocolate soufflé that had so completely and fully captured his attention.

"I was watching an episode of The Great Chefs of San Francisco and decided I wanted to make a soufflé," tells Costa, who grew up in Woodbridge, Virginia, and always remembers being interested in cooking. "So my mom and I went to the library and took out a book on soufflés and we made one."

The soufflé, Costa reports all these years later, did not fall, although he is quick to add they might have overcooked it a bit. Any eye for perfection and detail in the kitchen that no doubt still serves him well as the head chef of the always-busy Mediterranean small-plates José Andrés's restaurant, Zaytinya.

The simple yet striking Penn Quarter restaurant evokes the beauty of the Greek islands with its modern, airy feel and sea blue and pure white decor, while the menu takes its inspiration from Turkish, Greek, and Lebanese flavors. These two dishes serve as great examples of how the restaurant combines those food traditions while keeping them current. At Zaytinya, Costa uses a feta imported from Greece for the Htipiti, which is less salty and softer than the ones sold here. A heavier emphasis on salting stands as one of the keys to the brussels sprouts dish, Costa shares. The salt cuts the bitterness of the brussels sprouts, thereby allowing diners to truly enjoy the flavor of the vegetable that sometimes gets a bad rap. Clearly it works. The Brussels Sprouts Afelia holds the title as the most requested recipe at the Zaytinya.

701 9th Street NW, Washington, DC 20001, (202) 638-0800, zaytinya.com

HTIPITI
Serves 2

4 red bell peppers
1 clove garlic
1 shallot, peeled
3 tablespoons red wine vinegar
¼ cup extra-virgin olive oil
Dash white pepper
½ tablespoon salt
1½ tablespoons fresh thyme, stems removed
8 ounces block feta cheese

Preheat oven to 450°F. Place red peppers directly on oven racks. Bake for approximately 30 minutes, turning every 7 minutes or so. When the peppers are charred, remove from the oven carefully with tongs. Set the peppers aside and let the peppers cool. Mince garlic and shallots and place in a small mixing bowl. Combine oil, vinegar, garlic, shallots, white pepper, and salt. Set aside.

Peel the charred skin from the outside of the peppers. Discard the peels, stems, and seeds. Chop the peppers into small pieces and place in medium sized mixing bowl. Whisk dressing to combine and pour over peppers. Sprinkle fresh thyme on top of pepper mixture. Coarsely chop feta into small pieces and add to pepper mixture. Stir ingredients together and chill for 15 minutes before serving.

BRUSSELS SPROUTS AFELIA
Serves 4

FOR THE CORIANDER LADOLEMONO:

3 tablespoons whole coriander seeds
2 tablespoons Greek yogurt
2 tablespoons freshly squeezed lemon juice
½ cup extra-virgin olive oil

FOR THE ROASTED GARLIC YOGURT:

2 cloves roasted garlic
6 tablespoons of Greek yogurt
Sea salt to taste
¼ cup cranberries
½ cup port or other sweet wine
Olive oil for frying
1 pound brussels sprouts
Sea salt to taste
¼ cup chopped dill
2 tablespoons roasted garlic yogurt per serving
¼ cup coriander ladolemono per serving

To prepare the coriander ladolemono: Using a rolling pin, grind the coriander seeds until coarsely ground. Do not grind the seeds too finely. Whisk the coriander seeds into the Greek yogurt. Slowly add the lemon juice and olive oil and continue whisking until it forms a smooth, creamy dressing.

To prepare the roasted garlic yogurt: Using the back of a knife, mash the roasted garlic cloves. Mix into the yogurt and season with salt.

To assemble: In a small sauce pot, combine the cranberries and port. Heat over a medium flame until the port just begins to simmer. Remove from the heat and allow the cranberries to soak for 30 minutes. Remove the cranberries and reserve for the end of the recipe.

Preheat a heavy bottomed pot or deep fryer to 350°F.

Trim the ends of the brussels sprouts and discard. Remove any discolored leaves and cut into quarters.

Deep fry the brussels sprouts for about 2 minutes until golden. Do not overcook as the brussels sprouts will turn dark and become bitter. Remove from heat and drain.

Remove any excess oil with a paper towel. Toss brussels sprouts lightly with salt and chopped dill. Adjust salt to taste as needed.

To plate: On a serving plate, spread the roasted garlic yogurt on the bottom of the plate. Arrange the brussels sprouts on top of the yogurt. Top with coriander ladolemono dressing.

Garnish with rehydrated cranberries.

INDEX

ACKNOWLEDGEMENTS

Insert your best cliché here about needing many ingredients to create the perfect dish, and you begin to get the idea of the number people who helped cook up Great Food Finds Washington, DC. The main—and thankfully not so secret—ingredients among them are the many chefs of Washington DC who shared their recipes, stories, and insights with us. We feel beyond grateful to have been invited into your kitchens to watch first-hand the magic that often goes unseen. Thank you for graciously sharing your in-demand time and talent with us. And, thank you for allowing us to see and hear the many rich layers of memory, skill, practice, drive, and gift that you bring to the Washington, DC restaurant world. When I think back on what the restaurant scene looked like when I moved here in 1991, I am in disbelief at how lucky we are you're feeding this town. Thank you.

A skilled group of professionals have helped with everything from arranging photo shoots to scheduling interviews. Along with the chefs, we could also not have done it without your helpful hands e-mailing, dialing, and troubleshooting along the way. Many, many thanks to Jessica Botta, Sue-Jean Chun, Jetty-Jane Connor, Fleur Paysour, Meg Malloy, Simone Rathle, Raya Sfeir, Abby Steinbock, and Brenda Zaidman. Additional gratitude for DC Chef's Table help and continued support to: Anthony Hesselius and the team at Linda Roth Associates, Jennifer Motruk, Jennifer Resick Williams, Meaghan Donohoe, Cameron Feller, Heather Freeman, Scott Homstead, Lindley Thornburg Richardson, Renee Sharrow and her colleagues at the Park Hyatt, Amber Pfau, Sangeetha Sarma, Stephanie Salvador, Shayla Martin, Stephanie Betteker, Kate Manecke, Jennie Kuperstein, Jacqueline Herrera, Rachel Hayden, Molly J. Stephey, Miriam's Kitchen, Sunflower Bakery, Jordyn Lazar, Madeline Block, Atul Narain, Sean-Patrick Applegate, Tseday Gizaw, Sandra Holley, Neidra Holmstrom, and Nina Kocher. Also, thanks to folks at Dupont Circle FRESHFARM Market for allowing us to photograph at the always perfectly in season market.

A dream team of testers also have had their hands on these recipes. An industrial-sized thank you to my kitchen expert friends Elizabeth Sternberg and Laurie Moskowitz for your help, skill, and smart feedback. I so appreciate it. A special shout-out to Yoav Susskind, the youngest, and always enthusiastic, chef in the group, for lending your cooking talents to this project—you were an enormous help. When you open your own restaurant, please remember to invite me to opening night. And, thanks to Ilana Preuss for scouring all those markets for obscure ingredients for test runs in your kitchen.

I am once again incredibly grateful to Amy Lyons for continuing to give me the opportunities to write about the city I love. It's always good to work with you. Thank you to everyone at Rowman & Littlefield for all of your help with Great Food Finds Washington, DC and for all you do to turn a computer file into a book.

Not only did I have the gift of Elissa Forman's friendship during her time on this earth, she also gifted me my friendship with Emily Goodstein. A dear friend and favorite book collaborator, Emily is the talent responsible for the beautiful images in this book. Emily, once again it has been a pure delight to work with you. I am so glad we got the band back together and can't wait for our next gig. Thank you for photographing this road trip, and thank you for your support and friendship along the way.

I am beyond lucky that the three best people I know live under the same roof as me. Jeff, Gabe, and Miriam, it's hard to imagine loving your more than I already do but I bet that's happened since I typed this. Thank you for that. Thank you for being you. And, thank you for making me smile on and off deadline.

—BK

There is no sheetcake large enough to properly celebrate those who have helped make this book possible.

To the chefs, line cooks, farmers and producers, PR folks, front of house managers, hosts, servers, dishwashers and hardworking members of the Washington restaurant community, your stories of the new American dream inspire me. Thank you for all you do to keep our city well fed and happy.

Gratitude to Amy Lyons at Globe Pequot Press, thank you for, once again, believing I was the right photographer for this project.

Much appreciation to Molly Amster, Amy Born, Jeremy Bratt, Natalie Cole, Sara Fatell, Cara Fisher, Rebecca Goodstein, Betsy Gressler, Allison Grossman, Sally Heaven, Anthony Hesselius, Jodi Holzband, Beth Kurtz, Hanaa Rifaey, Sarah Rosenfeld, Jill Stepak, Caroline

Stuart-Freas and Amber Wobschall who drooled over preview photos, donned bee suits, made sure I didn't fall off of various chairs while trying to get the perfect angle and helped to curate our list of featured eateries.

Thank you for indulging my love of photography at such a young age, Mom and Dad... and for getting all of those photos I captured on film developed at the drugstore. If the number of "mirror selfies" of 8-year-old-Emily was any indication, the precursor to my photography career was not financially neutral.

Elissa Froman, who would have thought that Rosh Hashanah dinner in 2008 would lead to a friendship with Beth and two book collaborations, too? I miss you every day and love to imagine the long list of agenda items we would cover over the best slice of Goober Pie at Kramer's while wearing dangly earrings and festive scarves. Thank you for introducing me to Beth and leaving a community of activists, artists, and hilarious humans to tend to your memory.

Without you, Beth Kanter, my apartment would be beige and I would surely not be "self employed and loving it." Thank you for teaching me the art of breezy and once again inviting me along on this delicious adventure. Your patience, bravery, creativity and kindness make you a swell collaborator and a precious friend.

Finally, The Ron Kelly: You are as sweet and refreshing as a mango lassi. You are my favorite.

—EPG

ABOUT THE AUTHOR

BETH KANTER has written a number of books about her favorite city including *Day Trips from Washington, DC*; *Washington, DC Chef's Table*; *Food Lovers' Guide to Washington, DC*; and *No Access Washington, DC*. Her essays and articles have appeared in national newspapers, magazines, and online. Kanter has an MSJ from Northwestern's Medill School of Journalism and teaches writing workshops. Join her on Instagram at @beekaekae.

ABOUT THE PHOTOGRAPHER

EMILY PEARL GOODSTEIN is a digital strategy consultant, sheet cake enthusiast, photographer, and rabble rouser from Washington, DC. She loves oversharing on social media—follow along at @emilygoodstein for restaurant suggestions and other insider info. This is Emily's third book about her hometown in collaboration with Beth Kanter.